MONTESSORI
for
PARENTS

Maria Montessori was born in 1870, and she was the first woman ever granted a medical degree by an Italian university. As a child, she showed great ability in mathematics and originally intended to become an engineer. She did postgraduate work in psychiatry.

At the age of 28, Montessori became directress of a tax-supported school for defective children. Working thirteen hours a day *with the children,* she developed materials and methods which allowed them to perform reasonably well on school problems previously considered far beyond their capacity. Her great triumph, in reality and in the newspapers, came when she presented children from mental institutions at the public examinations for primary certificates, which was as far as the average Italian ever went in formal education — and her children passed the exam.

Typically, she drew from her experience the vigorous conclusion — that if *these* children could be brought to the academic levels reached by normal children, then there had to be something horribly wrong with the education of normal children. And so she moved on to the *normal* children of the slums. Thereafter, by her own desire and by public demand, she was an educator, not a medical doctor.

Montessori's insights and methods are contained in four basic texts, now republished: THE MONTESSORI METHOD, SPONTANEOUS ACTIVITY IN EDUCATION (*The Advanced Montessori Method,* volume 1), THE MONTESSORI ELEMENTARY MATERIAL (*The Advanced Montessori Method,* volume 2), and DR. MONTESSORI'S OWN HANDBOOK.

THE MONTESSORI METHOD, by Maria Montessori. Introduction by Martin Mayer. The education of children from 3 to 6. With all the original photographs. 50 photos/figures. 448 pages. $6.50

SPONTANEOUS ACTIVITY IN EDUCATION, by Maria Montessori. *The Advanced Montessori Method,* volume 1. The education of children from 7 to 11. 384 pages. $6.50

THE MONTESSORI ELEMENTARY MATERIAL, by Maria Montessori. *The Advanced Montessori Method,* volume 2. The education of children from 7 to 11. 116 photos/figures. 512 pages. $8.50

DR. MONTESSORI'S OWN HANDBOOK, by Maria Montessori. 43 photos/figures plus 1 four-color photo. 170 pages. $5.00

MONTESSORI FOR PARENTS, by Dorothy Canfield Fisher. 20 photos plus 1 four-color photo. 288 pages. $5.95

THE MONTESSORI MANUAL FOR TEACHERS AND PARENTS, by Dorothy Canfield Fisher. Practical exercises and lessons on the use of the apparatus in homes and schools, nature study, and an extended discussion on Montessori discipline and obedience. 15 photos plus 1 four-color photo. 154 pages. $5.00

NEW EDITIONS PUBLISHED BY
ROBERT BENTLEY, INC.
18 Pleasant St., Cambridge, Massachusetts 02139

Maria Montessori

MONTESSORI
for
PARENTS

by
DOROTHY CANFIELD FISHER

Author of *The Bent Twig, The Deepening Stream, Vermont Tradition — The Biography of an Outlook on Life, Understood Betsy, Made-To-Order Stories,* etc., etc.

WITH TWENTY PHOTOGRAPHS
ONE IN FOUR COLORS

1965
ROBERT BENTLEY, INC.
18 PLEASANT ST., CAMBRIDGE, MASSACHUSETTS 02139

DEDICATED
BY PERMISSION
TO
MARIA MONTESSORI

PREFACE

On my return recently from a somewhat prolonged stay in Rome, I observed that my family and circle of friends were in a very different state of mind from that usually found by the home-coming traveler. I was not depressed by the usual conscientious effort to appear interested in what I had seen; not once did I encounter the wavering eye and flagging attention which are such invariable accompaniments to anecdotes of European travel, nor the usual elated rebound into topics of local interest after a tribute to the miles I had traveled, in some such generalizing phrase of finality as, " Well, I suppose you enjoyed Europe as much as ever."

If I had ever suffered from the enforced repression within my own soul of my various European experiences I was more than indemnified by the reception which awaited this last return to my native land. For I found myself set upon and required to give an account of what I had seen, not only by my family and friends, but by callers, by acquaintances in the streets, by friends of acquaintances, by letters from people I knew, and many from those whose names were unfamiliar.

The questions they all asked were of a striking similarity, and I grew weary in repeating the same

answers, answers which, from the nature of the subject, could be neither categorical nor brief. How
many evenings have I talked from the appearance of
the coffee-cups till a very late bedtime, in answer to
the demand, " Now, you've been to Rome; you've seen
the Montessori schools. You saw a great deal of Dr.
Montessori herself and were in close personal relations with her. Tell us all about it. Is it really so
wonderful? Or is it just a fad? Is it true that the
children are allowed to do exactly as they please?
I should think it would spoil them beyond endurance.
Do they really learn to read and write so young?
And isn't it very bad for them to stimulate them so
unnaturally? And . . ." this was a never-failing
cry, " what is there in it for our children, situated
as we are? "

Staggered by the amount of explanation necessary
to give the shortest answers that would be intelligible
to these searching, but, on the whole, quite misdirected questions, I tried to put off my interrogators
with the excellent magazine articles which have ap-
peared on the subject, and with the translation of
Dr. Montessori's book. There were various objec-
tions to being relegated to these sources of information. Some of my inquisitors had been too doubtful
of the value of the perhaps over-heralded new ideas
to take the trouble to read the book with the close
and serious attention necessary to make anything out
of its careful and scientific presentation of its theories.
Others, quite honestly, in the breathless whirl of

American business, professional and social life, were too busy to read such a long work. Some had read it and emerged from it rather dazed by the technical terms employed, with the dim idea that something remarkable was going on in Italy of which our public education ought to take advantage, but without the smallest definite idea of a possible change in their treatment of their own youngsters. All had many practical questions to put, based on the difference between American and Italian life, questions which, by chance, had not been answered in the magazine articles.

I heard, moreover, in varying degree, from all the different temperaments, the common note of skepticism about the results obtained. Everyone hung on my first-hand testimony as an impartial eye-witness. "You are a parent like us. Will it really work?" they inquired with such persistent unanimity that the existence of a still unsatisfied craving for information seemed unquestionable. If so many people in my small personal circle, differing in no way from any ordinary group of educated Americans, were so actively, almost aggressively interested in hearing my personal account of the actual working of the new system, it seemed highly probable that other people's personal circles would be interested. The inevitable result of this reasoning has been the composition of this small volume, which can claim for partial expiation of its existence that it has no great pretensions to anything but timeliness.

I have put into it, not only an exposition, as practical as I can make it, of the technic of the method as far as it lies within the powers of any one of us fathers and mothers to apply it, but in addition I have set down all the new ideas, hopes, and visions which have sprung up in my mind as a result of my close contact with the new system and with the genius who is its founder. For ideas, hopes, and visions are as important elements in a comprehension of this new philosophy as an accurate knowledge of the use of the " geometric insets," and my talks with Dr. Montessori lead me to think that she feels them to be much more essential. Contact with the new ideas is not doing for us what it ought, if it does not act as a powerful stimulant to the whole body of our thought about life. It should make us think, and think hard, not only about how to teach our children the alphabet more easily, but about such fundamental matters as what we actually mean by moral life; whether we really honestly wish the spiritually best for our children, or only the materially best; why we are really in the world at all. In many ways, this " Montessori System " is a new religion which we are called upon to help bring into the world, and we cannot aid in so great an undertaking without considerable spiritual as well as intellectual travail.

The only way for us to improve our children's lives by the application of these new ideas is by meditating on them until we have absorbed their very essence and then by making what varying applications of them are necessary in the differing condition of our lives. I have set down, without apology, my own Americanized meditations on Dr. Montessori's Italian text, simply because I chance to be one of the first American mothers to come into close contact with her and her work, and as such may be of value to my fellows. I have, however, honestly labeled and pigeon-holed these meditations on the general philosophy of the system, and set them in separate chapters so that it should not be difficult for the most casual reader to select what he wishes to read, without being forced into social, philosophical, or ethical considerations. I confess that I shall be greatly disappointed if he takes too exclusive advantage of this opportunity, for I quite agree with the Italian founder of the system that its philosophical and ethical elements are those which have in them most promise for a new future for us all.

Finally, in spite of all my excuses for the undertaking, I seem to myself, now that I am fairly embarked upon it, very presumptuous in speaking at all upon such high and grave matters, fit only for the sure and enlightened handling of the specialist. But this is a subject differing from biology, physiological psychology, and philosophy (although the foundations of the system are laid deep in those sciences), inasmuch as its usefulness to the race depends upon its comprehension by the greatest possible number of ordinary human beings. I hearten myself by remembering that if it is not to remain an interesting and futile theory, it must be, in its broad outlines at least, understood and practised by just such people as I am. We must all collaborate. And here is the place to say that I consider this book a very tentative performance; and that I will be very grateful for suggestions from any of my readers which will help to make a second edition more useful and complete.

This volume of impressions, therefore, lays no claim to erudition. It is not written by a biologist for other biologists, by a philosopher for an audience of college professors, or by a professional pedagogue to enlighten school-superintendents. An ordinary American parent, desiring above all else the best possible chance for her children, addresses this message to the innumerable legion of her companions in that desire.

Grateful acknowledgment is made to Miss M. I. Batchelder and Miss Mary G. Gillmore, both of the Horace Mann School, for helpful suggestions; to Miss Anne E. George, who also read the manuscript; to Dr. Maria Montessori's book "The Montessori Method" (Frederick A. Stokes Company, New York); and to the House of Childhood, Inc., 200 Fifth Avenue, New York, for the use of illustrations.

CONTENTS

ILLUSTRATIONS

CHAPTER I

SOME INTRODUCTORY REMARKS ABOUT
PARENTS

AN observation often made by philosophic observers of our social organization is that the
tremendous importance of primary teachers is ri-
diculously underestimated. The success or failure
of the teachers of little children may not perhaps
determine the amount of information acquired later
in its educative career by each generation, but no one
can deny that it determines to a considerable extent
the character of the next generation, and character
determines practically everything worth considering
in the world of men. Yet the mind of the average
community admits this but haltingly. The teachers of
small children are paid more than they were, but still
far less than the importance of their work deserves,
and they are still regarded by the unenlightened majority as insignificant compared to those who impart
information to older children and adolescents, a class
of pupils which, in the nature of things, is vastly more
able to protect its own individuality from the character of the teacher.

But is there a thoughtful parent living who has not

quailed at the haphazard way in which Fate has pitchforked him into a profession greatly more important and enormously more difficult? For it is not quite fair to us to say that we chose the profession of parent with our eyes open when we repeated the words of the marriage service. It cannot be denied that every pair of fiancés know that probably they will have children, but this knowledge has about the same degree of first-hand vividness in their minds that the knowledge of ultimate certain death has in the mind of the average healthy young person: there is as little conscious preparation for the coming event in the one case as in the other. No, we have some right on our side, under the prevailing conditions of education about the facts of life, in claiming that we are tossed headlong by a force stronger than ourselves into a profession and a terrifying responsibility which many of us would never have had the presumption to undertake in cold blood. We might conceivably have undertaken to build railway bridges, even though the lives of multitudes depended on them; we might have become lawyers and settled people's material affairs for them or even, as doctors, settled the matter of their physical life or death; but to be responsible to God, to society, and to the soul in question for the health, happiness, moral growth, and usefulness of a human soul, what reflective parent among the whole army of us has not had moments of heartsick terror at the realization of what he has been set to do?

I say " moments " advisedly, for it must be admitted that most of us manage to forget pretty continually the alarming possibilities of our situation. In this we are imitating the curious actual indifference to peril which, from time immemorial, has been observed among those who are exposed to any danger which is very long continued. The incapacity of human nature to feel any strong emotion for a considerable length of time, even one connected with the supposedly sacrosanct instinct for self-preservation, is to be observed in the well-worn examples of people living on the sides of volcanoes, and of workers among machinery, who will not take the most elementary precautions against accidents if the precautions consume much time or thought. Consequently it is not surprising that, as a whole, parents are not only not stricken to the earth by the responsibilities of their situation, but as a class are singularly blind to their duties, and oddly difficult to move to any serious, continued consideration of the task before them. This attitude bears a close relation to the axiom which has only to be stated to win instant recognition from any self-analyzing human being, " We would rather lie down and die than *think!* " We cannot, as a rule, be forced to think really, seriously, connectedly, logically about the form of our government, about our social organization, about how we spend our lives, even about the sort of clothes we wear or the food we eat,—questions affecting our comfort so cruelly that they would make us reflect if anything could. But we ourselves are the only ones to

suffer from our refusal to use our minds fully and
freely on such subjects. It is intolerable that our
callous indifference and incurable triviality should
wreak themselves upon the helpless children com-
mitted to our care. The least we can do, if we will not
do our own thinking, is to accept, with all gratitude,
the thinking that someone else has done for us.

For there is one loop-hole of escape in our modern
world from this self-imprisonment in shiftless ways
of mental life, and that is the creation and wide diffusion of the scientific spirit. There is apparently in
human nature, along with this invincible repugnance
to use reason on matters closely connected with our
daily life, a considerable pleasure in ratiocination if
it is exercised on subjects sufficiently removed from
our personal sphere. The man who will eat hot mince-
pie and rarebit at two in the morning and cry out
upon the Fates as responsible for the inevitable
sequence of suffering, may be, often is, in his chem-
ical laboratory, or his surgical practice, or his bio-
logical research, an investigator of the strictest integrity of reasoning.

Reflection on this curious trait of human nature may
bring some restoration of self-respect to parents in
the face of the apparently astounding fact that most
of the great educators have been by no means parents
of large families, and a large proportion of them
have been childless. This but follows the usual ec-
centric route taken by discoveries leading to the
amelioration of conditions surrounding man. It was

not an inhabitant of a malarial district, driven to desperation by the state of things, who discovered the crime of the mosquito. That discovery was made by men working in laboratories not in the least incommoded by malaria. Hundreds of generations of devoted mothers, ready and willing to give the last drop of their blood for their children's welfare, never discovered that unscalded milk-bottles are like prussic acid to babies. Childless workers in white laboratory aprons, standing over test-tubes, have revolutionized the physical hygiene of infancy and brought down the death-rate of babies beyond anything ever dreamed of by our parents.

But let it be remembered as comfort, exhortation, and warning to us that the greatest army of laboratory workers ever financed by a twentieth-century millionaire, would have been of no avail if the parents of the babies of the world had not taken to scalding the milk-bottles. Let us insist upon the recognition of our merit, such as it is. We will not, apparently we cannot, do the hard, consecutive, logical, investigating thinking which is the only thing necessary in many cases to better the conditions of our daily life; but we are not entirely impervious to reason, inasmuch as the world has seen us in this instance following, with the most praiseworthy docility, the teachings of those who have thought for us. The milk-bottles in by far the majority of American homes are really being scalded to-day; and " cholera morbus," " second summers," " teething fevers," and the like are becoming as out-of-date as " fever 'n' ague," " galloping consumption," and the like.

The lessened death-rate among babies is not only the most heartening spectacle for lovers of babies, but for hopers and believers in the general advancement of the race. This miraculous revolution in the care of infants under a year of age has taken place in less than a human generation. The grandparents of our children are still with us to pooh-pooh our sterilizings, and to look on with bewilderment while we treat our babies as intelligently as stock-breeders treat their animals. Let us take heart of grace. If scientific methods of physical hygiene in the care of children can be thus quickly inculcated, it is certainly worth while to storm the age-old redoubts sheltering the no less hoary abuses of their intellectual and spiritual treatment.

A scientist of another race, taking advantage of the works of all the other investigators along the same line (works which nothing could have induced us to study), laboring in a laboratory of her own invention, has been doing our hard, consecutive, logical, investigating thinking for us. Let us have the grace to take advantage of her discoveries, many of which have been stumbled upon from time to time in a haphazard, unformulated way by the instinctive wisdom of experience, but the synthesis of which into a coherent, usable system, with a consistent philosophical foundation, has been left to a childless scientific investigator.

CHAPTER II

A DAY IN A CASA DEI BAMBINI

I HAD not seen a Montessori school when I first read through Dr. Montessori's book. I laid it down with the mental comments, "All very well to write about! But, of course, it can't work anything like that in actual practice. Everyone knows that a child's party of only five or six children of that age (from two and a half to six) is seldom carried through without some sort of quarrel, even though an equal number of mothers are present, devoting themselves to giving the tots exactly whatever they want. It stands to reason that twenty or thirty children of that tender age, shut up together all day long and day after day, must, if they are normal children, have a great many healthy normal battles with each other!"

After putting myself in a dispassionate and judicial frame of mind by laying down these fixed preconceptions, I went to visit the Casa dei Bambini in the Franciscan Nunnery on the Via Giusti.

I half turn away in anticipatory discouragement from the task of attempting, for the benefit of American readers, any description of what I saw there. They will not believe it. I know they will not, because I myself, before I saw it with my own eyes,

7

would have discounted largely the most moderate statements on the subject. But even though stay-at-home people in other centuries may have salted liberally the tall stories of old-time travelers, they certainly had a taste for hearing them; and so possibly my plain account of what I saw that day may be read, even though it be to the accompaniment of incredulous exclamations.

My first glimpse was of a gathering of about twenty-five children, so young that several of them looked like real babies to me. I found afterwards that the youngest was just under three, and the oldest just over six. They were scattered about over a large, high-ceilinged, airy room, furnished with tiny, lightly-framed tables and chairs which, however, by no means filled the floor. There were big tracts of open space, where some of the children knelt or sat on light rugs. One was lying down on his back, kicking his feet in the air. A low, cheerful hum of conversation filled the air.

As my companion and I came into the room I noticed first that there was not that stiffening into self-consciousness which is the inevitable concomitant of " visitors " in our own schoolrooms. Most of the children, absorbed in various queer-looking tasks, did not even glance up as we entered. Others, apparently resting in the intervals between games, looked over across the room at us, smiled welcomingly as I would at a visitor entering my house, and a little group near us ran up with outstretched hands, saying with a pleas-

The School Room in the Convent of the Franciscan Nuns in the Via Giusti.

ant accent of good-breeding, "Good-morning!
Good-morning!" They then instantly went off about
their own affairs, which were evidently of absorbing
interest, for after that, except for an occasional
friendly look or smile, or a momentary halt by my
side to show me something, none of the little scholars
paid the least attention to me.

Now I myself, like all the American matrons of my
circle of acquaintances, am laboring conscientiously
to teach my children " good manners," but I decided,
on the instant, nothing would induce me to collect
twenty children of our town and have a Montessori
teacher enter the room to be greeted by them. The
contrast would be too painful. These were mostly
children of very poor, ignorant, and utterly untrained parents, and ours are children of people who
flatter themselves that they are the opposite of all
that; but I shuddered to think of the long silent,
discourteous stare which is the only recognition of
the presence of a visitor in our schools. And yet I
felt at once that I was attaching too much importance to a detail, the merest trifle, the slightest,
most superficial indication of the life beneath. We
Anglo-Saxons notice too acutely, I thought, these sur-
face differences of manner.

But, on the other hand, I was forced to consider
that I knew from bitter experience that children of
that age are still near enough babyhood to be absolutely primeval in their sincerity, and that it is practically impossible to make them, with any certainty

of the result, go through a form of courtesy which they do not feel genuinely. Also I observed that no one had pushed the children towards us, as I push mine, toward a chance visitor, with the command accompanied by an inward prayer for obedience, " Go and shake hands with Mrs. Blank."

In fact, I noticed it for the first time, there seemed no one there to push the children or to refrain from doing it. That collection of little tots, most of them too busy over their mysterious occupations even to talk, seemed, as far as a casual glance over the room went, entirely without supervision. Finally, from a corner, where she had been sitting (on the floor apparently) beside a child, there rose up a plainly-dressed woman, the expression of whose quiet face made almost as great an impression on me as the children's greetings had. I had always joined with heartfelt sympathy in the old cry of " Heaven help the poor teachers! " and in our town, where we all know and like the teachers personally, their exhausted condition of almost utter nervous collapse by the end of the teaching year is a painful element in our community life. But I felt no impulse to sympathize with this woman with untroubled eyes who, perceiving us for the first time, came over to shake hands with us. Instead, I felt a curious pang of envy, such as once or twice in my sentimental and stormy girlhood I felt at the sight of the peaceful face of a nun. I am now quite past the possibility of envying the life of a nun, but I must admit that it suddenly oc-

curred to me, as I looked at that quiet, smiling Italian
woman, that somehow my own life, for all its full
happiness, must lack some element of orderliness, of
discipline, of spiritual economy which alone could
have put that look of calm certainty on her face.
It was not the passive, changeless peace that one sees
in the eyes of some nuns, but a sort of rich, full-
blooded confidence in life.

She lingered beside us some moments, chatting with
my companion, who was an old friend of hers, and
who introduced her as Signorina Ballerini. I noticed
that she happened to stand all the time with her
back to the children, feeling apparently none of
that lion-tamer's instinct to keep an hypnotic eye
on the little animals which is so marked in our in-
structors. I can remember distinctly that there was
for us school-children actually a different feel to the
air and a strange look on the familiar school-furniture
during those infrequent intervals when the teacher
was called for an instant from the room and left us,
as in a suddenly rarefied atmosphere, giddy with the
removal of the pressure of her eye; but when this
teacher turned about casually to face the room again,
these children did not seem to notice either that she
had stopped looking at them or that she was now
doing it again.

We used to know, as by a sixth sense, exactly
where, at any moment, the teacher was, and a sudden
movement on her part would have made us all start
as violently and as instinctively as little chicks at

the sudden shadow of a hawk . . . and this, although we were often very fond indeed of our teachers. Remembering this, I noticed with surprise that
often, when one of these little ones lifted his face
from his work to ask the teacher a question, he had
been so unconscious of her presence during his concentration on his enterprise that he did not know
in the least where to look, and sent his eager eyes rov-
ing over the big room in a search for her, which ended
in such a sudden flash of joy at discovering her that
I felt again a pang of envy for this woman who had so
many more loving children than I have.

What could be these " games " which so absorbed
these children, far too young for any possibility of
pretense on their part? Moving with the unhampered, unobserved ease which is the rule in a
Montessori schoolroom, I began walking about, looking more closely at what the children were holding,
and I could have laughed at the simplicity of
many of the means which accomplished the apparent
miracle of self-imposed order and discipline before me . . . if I had not been ready to cry
at my own stupidity for not thinking of them myself. One little boy about three and a half years
old had been intent on some operation ever since we
had entered the room, and even now as I drew near
his little table and chair, he only glanced up for an
instant's smile without stopping the action of his
fingers. I leaned over him, hoping that the device
which so held his attention was not too complicated

for my inexperienced, unpedagogical mind to take in.
He was holding a light wooden frame about eighteen
inches square, on which were stretched two pieces of
cotton cloth, meeting down the middle like the joining
of a garment. On one of these edges was a row of
buttonholes and on the other a row of large bone
buttons. The child was absorbed in buttoning and
unbuttoning those two pieces of cloth.

He was new at the game, that was to be seen by the
clumsy, misdirected motions of his baby fingers, but
the process of his improvement was so apparent as,
his eyes shining with interest, he buttoned and un-
buttoned steadily, slowly, without an instant's inter-
ruption, that I watched him, almost as fascinated as
he. A child near us, apparently playing with blocks,
upset them with a loud noise, but my buttoning boy,
wrapped in his magic cloak of concentration, did not
so much as raise his eyes. I myself could not look
away, and as I gazed I thought of the many times a
little child of mine had tried to learn the secret of the
innumerable fastenings which hold her clothes together and how I, with the kindest impulse in the
world, had stopped her fumbling little fingers saying,
" No, dear, Mother can do that so much better. Let
Mother do it." It occurred to me now that the situation was very much as if, in the midst of a fascinating game of billiards, a professional player had
snatched the cue from my husband's hands, saying,
" You just stand and watch me do this. I can do it
much better than you."

The child before me stopped his work a moment and looked down at his little cotton waist. There was a row of buttons there, smaller but of the same family as those on the frame. As he gazed down, absorbed, at them, I could see a great idea dawn in his face. I leaned forward. He attacked the middle button, using with startling exactitude of imitation the same motion he had learned on his frame. But this button was not so large or so well placed. He had to bend his head over, his fingers were cramped, he made several movements backward. But then suddenly the first half of his undertaking was accomplished. The button was on one side, the buttonhole on the other. I held my breath. He set to work again. The cloth slipped from his boneless little fingers, the button twisted itself awry, I fairly ached with the idiotic habit of years of interference to snatch it and do it for him. And then I saw that he was slowly forcing it into place. When the bone disk finally shone out, round and whole, on the far side of the buttonhole, the child drew a long breath and looked up at me with so ecstatic a face of triumph that I could have shouted, " Hurrah! " Then, without paying any more attention to me, he rose, sauntered over to a corner of the room where a thick piece of felt covered the floor, and lay down on his back, his hands clasped under his head, gazing with tranquil, reposeful vacuity at the ceiling. He was resting himself after accomplishing a great step forward. I did not fail to notice that, except for my

entirely fortuitous observation of his performance,
nobody had seen his absorption any more than they
now saw his apparent idleness.

I tucked all these observations away in a corner of
my mind for future reflection, and moved on to the
nearest child, a little girl, perhaps a year older than
the boy, who was absorbed as eagerly as he over a
similar light wooden frame, covered with two pieces
of cloth. But these were fastened together with pieces
of ribbon which the child was tying and untying.
There was no fumbling here. As rapidly, as deftly,
with as careless a light-hearted ease as a pianist running over his scales, she was making a series of the
flattest, most regular bow-knots, much better, I knew
in my heart, than I could accomplish at anything like
that speed. Although she had advanced beyond the
stage of intent struggle with her material, her interest and pleasure in her own skill was manifest. She
looked up at me, and then smiled proudly down at
her flying fingers.

Beyond her another little boy, with a leather-
covered frame, was laboriously inserting shoe-buttons
into their buttonholes with the aid of an ordinary
button-hook. As I looked at him, he left off, and
stooping over his shoes, tried to apply the same system to their buttons. That was too much for him.
After a prolonged struggle he gave it up for the
time, returning, however, to the buttons on his frame
with entirely undiminished ardor.

Next to him sat a little girl, with a pile of small

pieces of money before her on her tiny table. She was engaged in sorting these into different piles according to their size, and, though I stood by her some time, laughing at the passion of accuracy which fired her, she was so absorbed that she did not even notice my presence. As I turned away I almost stumbled over a couple of children sitting on the floor, engaged in some game with a variety of blocks which looked new to me. They were ten squared rods of equal thickness, of which the shortest looked to be a tenth the length of the longest, and the others of regularly diminishing lengths between these two extremes. These were painted in alternate stripes of red and blue, these stripes being the same width as the shortest rod. The children were putting these together in consecutive order so as to make a sort of series, and although they were evidently much too young to count, they were aiding themselves by touching with their fingers each of the painted stripes, and verifying in this way the length of the rod. I could not follow this process, although it was plainly something arithmetical, and turned to ask the teacher about it.

I saw her across the room engaged in tying a bandage about a child's eyes. Wondering if this were some new, scientific form of punishment, I stepped to that part of the room and watched the subsequent proceedings. The child, his lips curved in an expectant smile, even laughing a little in pleasant excitement, turned his blindfolded face to a pile of small pieces of cloth

before him. Several children, walking past, stopped
and hung over the edge of his desk with lively interest.
The boy drew out from the pile a piece of velvet.
He felt of this intently, running the sensitive tips of
his fingers lightly over the nap, and cocking his head
on one side in deep thought. The child-spectators
gazed at him with sympathetic attention. When he
gave the right name, they all smiled and nodded
their heads in satisfaction. He drew out another
piece from the big pile, coarse cotton cloth this time,
which he instantly recognized; then a square of satin
over which his little finger-tips wandered with evident
sensuous pleasure. His successful naming of this was
too much for his envious little spectators. They
turned and fled toward the teacher and when I reached
her, she was the center of a little group of children,
all clamoring to be blindfolded.

"How they do love that exercise!" she said, looking after them with shining eyes . . . I could have
sworn, with mother's eyes!

"Are you too busy and hurried," I asked, "to explain to me the game those children are playing with
the red and blue rods?"

She answered with some surprise, "Oh, no, I'm
not busy and hurried at all!" (quite as though we
were not all living in the twentieth century) and went
on, "The children can come and find me if they need
me."

So I had my first lesson in the theory of self-
education and self-dependence underlying the Mon-

tessori apparatus, to the accompaniment of occasional requests for aid, or demands for sympathy over an achievement, made in clear, baby treble. That theory will be taken up later in this book, as this chapter is intended only to be a plain narration of a few of the sights encountered by an ordinary observer in a morning in a Montessori school.

After a time I noticed that four little girls were sitting at a neatly-ordered small table, spread with a white cloth, apparently eating their luncheons. The teacher, in answer to my inquiring glance at them, explained that it was their turn to be the waitresses that day, for the children's lunch, and so they ate their own meal first.

She was called away just then, and I sat looking at the roomful of busy children, listening to the pleasant murmur of their chats together, watching them move freely about as they liked, noting their absorbed, happy concentration on their tasks. Already some of the sense of the miraculous which had been so vivid in my mind during my first survey of the school was dulled, or rather, explained away. Now that I had seen some of the details composing the picture, the whole seemed more natural. It was not surprising, for instance, that the little girl sorting the pieces of money should not instead be pulling another child's hair, or wandering in aimless and potentially naughty idleness about the room. It was not necessary either to force or exhort her to be a quiet and untroublesome citizen of that little republic. She

would no more leave her fascinating occupation to
go and " be naughty " than a professor of chemistry
would leave an absorbing experiment in his laboratory to go and rob a candy-store. In both cases it
would be leaving the best sort of a " good time " for
a much less enjoyable undertaking.

In the midst of these reflections (my first glimmer
of understanding of what it was all about), a lively
march on the piano was struck up. Not a word was
spoken by the teacher, indeed I had not yet heard her
voice raised a single time to make a collective re-
mark to the whole body of children, but at once, acting on the impulse which moves us all to run down the
street towards the sound of a brass band, most of the
children stopped their work and ran towards the open
floor-space near the piano. Some of the older ones,
of five, formed a single-file line, which was rapidly
recruited by the monkey-like imitativeness of the little
ones, into a long file. The music was martial, the
older children held their heads high and stamped
loudly as they marched about, keeping time very accurately to the strongly marked rhythm of the tune.
The little tots did their baby best to copy their big
brothers and sisters, some of them merely laughing
and stamping up and down without any reference to
the time, others evidently noticing a difference between their actions and those of the older ones, and
trying to move their feet more regularly.

No one had suggested that they leave their work-
tables to play in this way (indeed a few too absorbed

to heed the call of the music still hung intently over their former occupations), no one suggested that they step in time to the music, no one corrected them when they did not. The music suddenly changed from a swinging marching air to a low, rhythmical croon. The older children instantly stopped stamping and began trotting noiselessly about on their tiptoes, imitated again as slavishly as possible by the admiring smaller ones. The uncertain control of their equilibrium by these littler ones, made them stagger about, as they practised this new exercise, like the little bacchantes, intoxicated with rhythm, which their glowing faces of delight seemed to proclaim them.

I was penetrated with that poignant, almost tearful sympathy in their intense enjoyment which children's pleasure awakens in every adult who has to do with them. "Ah, what a *good* time they are having!" I cried to myself, and then reflected that they had been having some sort of very good time ever since I had come into the room. And yet even my unpractised eye could see a difference between this good time and the kindergarten, charming as that is to watch. No prettily-dressed, energetic, thoroughgoing young lady had beckoned the children away from their self-chosen occupations. There was no set circle here with the lovely teacher in the middle, and every child's eyes fastened constantly on her nearly always delightful but also overpoweringly developed adult personality. There was no set " game " being played, the discontinuation of which depended on the teacher's more or less accurate guess at when the children were becoming tired. Indeed, as I reflected on this, I noticed that, although the bigger ones were continuing their musical march with undiminished pleasure, the younger ones had already exhausted the small amount of consecutive interest their infant organisms are capable of, and, without spoiling the fun for the others, indeed without being observed, had suddenly stopped dancing and prancing as suddenly as they began and, with the kitten-like fitfulness of their age, were wandering away in groups of two and three out to the great, open courtyard.

I suppose they went on playing quieter games there, but I did not follow them, so absorbed was I in watching the four little girls who had now at last finished their very leisurely meal and were preparing the tables for the other children. They were about four and a half and five years old, an age at which I would have thought children as capable of solving a problem in calculus as of undertaking, without supervision, to set tables for twenty other babies. They went at their undertaking with no haste, indeed with a slowness which my racial impatience found absolutely excruciating. They paused constantly for prolonged consultations, and to verify and correct themselves as they laid the knife, fork, spoon, plate, and napkin at each place. Interested as I was, and beginning, as I did, to understand a little of the ideas of the school, I still was so under the domination of my lifetime of over-emphasis on the importance of the immediate result of an action, that I felt the same impulse I had restrained with difficulty beside the buttoning boy—to snatch the things from their incompetent little hands and whisk them into place on the tables.

But then I noticed that the clock showed only a little after eleven, and that evidently the routine of the school was planned expressly so that there would be no need for haste.

The phrase struck my mental ear curiously, and arrested my attention. I reflected on that condition with the astonished awe of a modern, meeting it almost for the first time. " No need for haste "—it was like being transported into the timeless ease of eternity.

And then I fell to asking myself why there was always so much need for haste in my own life and in that of my children? Was it, after all, so necessary? What were we hurrying so to accomplish? I remembered my scorn of the parties of Cook's tourists, clattering into the Sistine Chapel for a momentary glance at the achievement of a lifetime of genius, painted on the ceiling, and then galloping out again for a hop-skip-and-jump race down through the Stanze of Raphael. It occurred to me, disquietingly, that possibly, instead of really training my children, I might be dragging them headlong on a Cook's tour through life. It also occurred to me that if the Montessori ideas were taken up in my family, the children would not be the only ones to profit by them.

The Meal Hour.

When I emerged from this brown study, the little
girls had finished their task and there stood before
me tables set for twenty little people, set neatly and
regularly, without an item missing. The children,
called in from their play in the courtyard, came
marching along (they do take collective action when
collective interests genuinely demand it) and sat down
without suggestions, each, I suppose, at the place he
had occupied while working at those same tiny tables.
I held my breath to see the four little waitresses enter
the room, each carrying a big tureen full of hot soup.
I would not have trusted a child of that age to carry
a glass of water across a room. The little girls advanced slowly, their eyes fixed on the contents of
their tureens, their attention so concentrated on their
all-important enterprise that they seemed entirely ob-
livious of the outer world. A fly lighted on the nose
of one of these solemnly absorbed babies. She twisted
the tip of that feature, making the most grotesque
grimaces in her effort to dislodge the tickling in-
truder, but not until she had reached a table and set
down her sacred tureen in safety, did she raise her
hand to her face. I revised on the instant all my
fixed convictions about the innate heedlessness and
lack of self-control of early childhood; especially as
she turned at once to her task of ladling out the
soup into the plates of the children at her table, a
feat which she accomplished as deftly as any adult
could have done.

The napkins were unfolded, the older children

tucked them under their chins and began to eat their soup. The younger ones imitated them more or less handily, though with some the process meant quite a struggle with the napkin. One little boy, only one in all that company, could not manage his. After wrestling with it, he brought it to the teacher, who had dropped down on a chair near mine. So sure was I of what her action inevitably would be, that I fairly felt my own hands automatically follow hers in the familiar motions of tucking a napkin under a child's round chin.

I cannot devise any way to set down on paper with sufficient emphasis the fact that she did not tuck that napkin in. She held it up in her hands, showed the child how to take hold of a larger part of the corner than he had been grasping, and, illustrating on herself, gave him an object-lesson. Then she gave it back to him. He had caught the idea evidently, but his undisciplined little fingers, out of sight there, under his chin, would not follow the direction of his brain, though that was evidently, from the grave intentness of his baby face, working at top speed. With a sigh, that irresistible sigh of the little child, he took out the crumpled bit of linen and looked at it sadly. I clasped my hands together tightly to keep them from flying at him and accomplishing the operation in a twinkling. Why, the poor child's soup was getting cold!

Again I wish to reiterate the statement that the teacher did not tuck that napkin in. She took it once more and went through very slowly all the necessary movements. The child's big, black eyes fastened on her in a passion of attention, and I noticed that his little empty hands followed automatically the slow, distinctly separated, analyzed movements of the teacher's hands. When she gave the napkin back to him, he seized it with an air of resolution which would have done honor to Napoleon, grasping it firmly and holding his wandering baby-wits together with the aid of a determined frown. He pulled his collar away from his neck with one hand and, still frowning determinedly, thrust a large segment of the napkin down with the other, spreading out the remainder on his chest, with a long sigh of utter satisfaction, which went to my heart. As he trotted back to his place, I noticed that the incident had been observed by several of the children near us, on whose smiling faces, as they looked at their triumphant little comrade, I could see the reflection of my own gratified sympathy. One of them reached out and patted the napkin as its proud wearer passed.

But I had not been all the morning in that children's home, perfect, though not made with a mother's hands, without having my mother's jealousy sharply aroused. A number of things had been stirring up protests in my mind. I was alarmed at the sight of all these babies, happy, wisely occupied, perfectly good, and learning unconsciously the best sort of lessons, and yet in an atmosphere differing so entirely from all my preconceived ideas of a home. All

this might be all very well for Italian mothers so poor
that they were obliged to leave their children in order
to go out and help earn the family living; or for English mothers, who expect as a matter of course that
their little children shall spend most of their time with
nurse-maids and governesses. But I could not spare
my children, I told myself. I asked nothing better
than to have them with me every moment they were
awake. What was to be done about this ominously
excellent institution which seemed to treat the children more wisely than I, for all my efforts? I felt an
uneasy, apprehensive hostility towards these methods,
contrasting so entirely with mine, for mine were, I
assured myself hotly, based on the most absolute,
supreme mother's love for the child.

I now turned to the teacher and said protestingly,
" That would have been a very little thing to do for
a child."

She laughed. " I'm not his nurse-maid. I'm his
teacher," she replied.

" That's all very well, but his soup *will* be cold, you
know, and he will be late to his luncheon! "

She did not deny this, but she did not seem as struck
as I was by the importance of the fact. She answered
whimsically, " Ah, one must remember not to obtrude
one's adult materialism into the idealistic world of
children. He is so happy over his victory over
himself that he wouldn't notice if his soup were
iced."

" But warm soup is a good thing, a very good

THE MORNING CLEAN-UP.

WAITER CARRYING SOUP.

thing," I insisted, " and you have literally robbed
him of his. More than that, I seem to see that all
this insistence on self-dependence for children must
interfere with a great many desirable regularities of
family life."

She looked at me indulgently. " Yes, warm soup
is a good thing, but is it such a very important thing?
According to our adult standards it is more palatable,
but it's really about as good food if eaten cold, isn't
it? And, anyhow, he eats it cold only this once.
You'd snatch him away from his plate of warm soup
without scruple if you thought he was sitting in a
draught and would take cold. Isn't his moral health
as important as his physical? "

" But it might be very inconvenient for someone
else, in an ordinary home, to wait so interminably for
him to learn to wait on himself."

Her answer was a home-thrust. " If it's too much
trouble to give him the best conditions at home,
wouldn't he be better sent to a Casa dei Bambini,
which has no other aim than to have things just right
for his development? "

This silenced me for a time. I turned away, but
was recalled by her remarking, " Besides, I've put him
more in the way of getting his soup hot from now on,
than you would, by tucking in his napkin and sending him back at once. To-day's plateful would have
been warm; but how about to-morrow and the day
after, and so on, unless you, or some other grown-
up happened to be at hand to wait on him. And

on my part, what could I do, if all twenty-five of the children were helpless? "

I seized on this opportunity to voice some of the mother's jealousy which underlay all my extreme admiration and astonishment at the sights of the morning, " If you didn't keep such an octopus clutch on the children, separating them all day in this way from their own families, if they were sent home to eat their luncheons, why, there would be mothers enough to go around. *They* would be only too glad to tuck the little napkins in! "

The teacher looked at me, level-browed, and said, with a dry, enigmatic accent which made me reflect uneasily, long afterwards, on her words, " They certainly would. Do you really think that would be an improvement? "

CHAPTER III

MORE ABOUT WHAT HAPPENS IN A CASA DEI BAMBINI

O F course one day's observations do not give even a bird's-eye view of all the operations of a Montessori school, and this chapter is intended to supplement somewhat the very incomplete survey of the last and to touch at least, in passing, upon some of the other important activities in which the children are engaged. If this description seems lacking in continuity and uniformity, it represents all the more faithfully the impressions of an observer of a Casa dei Bambini. For there one sees no trace of the slightly Prussian uniformity of action to which we are accustomed in even the freest of our primary schools and kindergartens. You need not expect at ten o'clock to hear the " ten-o'clock class in reading," for possibly on that day no child will happen to feel like reading. You need not think that the teacher will call up the star pupil to have him write for you. He may be lying on the floor absorbed in an arithmetical game and a Montessori teacher would as soon blow up her schoolroom with dynamite as interfere with the natural direction, taken for the moment by the self-educating instincts of her children.

In planning a visit to a Casa dei Bambini, you can
be sure of only one thing, not, however, an incon-
siderable thing, and that is that all the children will
be happily absorbed in some profitable undertaking.
It never fails. There are no " blue Mondays." Rain
or shine outdoors, inside the big room there always
blows across the heart of the visitor a fine, tonic
breath of free, and hence, never listless life. On days
in winter when the sirocco blows, the debilitating
wind from Africa, which reduces the whole population
of Rome to inert and melancholy passivity, the children in the Casa are perhaps not quite so briskly
energetic as usual in their self-imposed task of teaching and governing themselves, but they are by far the
most briskly energetic Romans in the city.

It is all so interesting to them, they cannot stop to
be bored or naughty. Just as one of our keen,
hungry-minded Yankee school-teachers, turned loose
for the first time in an historic European city, throws
herself with such fervor into the exploration of all
its fascinating and informing sights that she is astonished to hear later that it was one of the hottest
and most trying summers ever known, so these equally
hungry-minded, healthy children fling themselves upon
the fascinating and informing wonders of the world
about them with such ardor that they are always
astonished when the long, happy day is done.

The freedom accorded them is absolute, the only
rule being that they must not hurt or annoy others,
a rule which, after the first brief chaos at the begin-

ning, when the school is being organized, is always
respected with religious care by these little citizens;
although to call a Montessori school a " little republic " and the children " little citizens," gives much too
formal an idea of the free-and-easy, happily unforced
and natural relations of the children with each other.
The phrase Casa dei Bambini is being translated
everywhere nowadays by English-speaking people as
" The House of Childhood," whereas its real meaning,
both linguistic and spiritual, is, " The Children's
Home."

That is what it is, a real home for *children*, where
everything is arranged for their best interests, where
the furniture is the right size for them, where there
are no adult occupations going on to be interrupted
and hindered by the mere presence of the children,
where there are no rules made solely to facilitate life
for grown-ups, where children, without incurring the
reproach (expressed or tacit) of disturbing their
elders, can freely and joyously, and if they please,
noisily, develop themselves by action from morning to
night. With the removal by this simple means of most
of the occasions for friction in the life of little children, it is amazing to see how few, how negligibly
few occasions there are for naughtiness. The great
question of discipline which so absorbs us all, solves
itself, melts into thin air, becomes non-existent. Each
child gives himself the severest sort of self-discipline
by his interest in his various undertakings. He
learns self-control as a by-product of his healthy

absorption in some fascinating pursuit, or as a result of his instinctive imitation of older children.

For instance, no adult was obliged to shout commandingly to the little-girl waitress not to drop her soup-tureen to brush the fly from her nose. She was so filled with the pride of her responsible position that she obeyed the same inner impulse towards self-control which induces adult self-sacrifice. On the other hand, the buttoning boy did not refrain by a similar, violent effort of his will from snatching the blocks from the arithmetical children. It simply never occurred to him, so happily absorbed was he in his own task.

I asked, of course, the question which obsesses every new observer in a Children's Home, " But what do you do, with all this fine theory of absolute freedom, when a child *is* naughty? Sometimes, even if not often, you surely must encounter the kicking, screaming, snatching, hair-pulling ' bad ' child! " I was told then that the health of such a child is looked into at once, such perverted violence being almost certainly the result of deranged physical condition. If nothing pathological can be discovered, he is treated as a morally sick child, given a little table by himself, from which he can look on at the cheerful, ordered play of the schoolroom, allowed any and all toys he desires, petted, soothed, indulged, pitied, but (of course this is the vital point) severely let alone by the other children, who are told that he is " sick " and so cannot play with them until he gets well. This quiet isolation, with its object-lesson of good-natured play among the other children, has a hypnotically calming effect, the child's "naughtiness" for very lack of food to feed upon, or resistance to blow its flames, disappears and dies away.

This, I say, was the explanation given me at first, but later, when I came to know more intimately the little group of Montessori enthusiasts in Rome, I learned more about the matter. One of my Montessori friends told me laughingly, " We found that nobody would believe us at all when we told the simple truth, when we said that we never, literally never, do encounter that hypothetical, ferociously naughty, small child. They look at us with such an obvious incredulity that, for the honor of the system, we had to devise some expedient. So we ransacked our memories for one or two temporary examples of ' badness ' which we met at first before the system was well organized, and remembered how we had dealt with them. Now, when people ask us what we do when the children begin to scratch and kick each other, instead of insisting that children as young as ours, when properly interested, never do these things, we tell them the old story of our device of years ago."

I have said that the real translation for Casa dei Bambini is The Children's Home, and I feel like insisting upon this rendering, which gives us so much more idea of the character of the institution. At least, from now on, in this book, that English phrase will be used from time to time to designate a Montes-

sori school. It is, for instance, their very own home
not only in the sense that it is a place arranged spe-
cially for their comfort and convenience, but furthermore a place for which they feel that steadying sense
of responsibility which is one of the greatest moral
advantages of a home over a boarding-house, a moral
advantage of home life which children in ordinary
circumstances are rarely allowed to share with their
elders. They are boarders (though gratuitous ones)
with their father and mother, and, as a natural consequence, they have the remote, detached, unsympathetic aloofness from the problem of running the
house which is characteristic of the race of boarders.

In the Casa dei Bambini this is quite different. Because it is their home and not a school, the hours are
very long, practically all the day being spent there.
The children have the responsibility not only for their
own persons, but for the care of their Home. They
arrive early in the morning and betake themselves at
once to the small washstands with pitchers and bowls
of just the size convenient for them to handle. Here
they make as complete a morning toilet as anyone
could wish, washing their faces, necks, hands, and
ears (and behind the ears!), brushing their teeth,
making manful efforts to comb their hair, cleaning
their finger-nails with scrupulous care, and helping
each other with fraternal sympathy. It is astonishing (for anyone who had the illusion that she knew
child-nature) to note the contrast between the vivid
purposeful attention they bestow on all these proc-

esses when they are allowed to do them for themselves, and the bored, indifferent impatience we all
know so well when it is our adult hands which are
doing all the work. The big ones (of five and six)
help the little ones, who, eager to be " big ones "
in their turn, struggle to learn as quickly as possible
how to do things for themselves.

After the morning toilet of the children is finished,
it is the turn of the schoolroom. The fresh-faced,
shining-eyed children scatter about the big room,
with tiny brushes and dust-pans and little brooms.
They attack the corners where dust lurks, they dust
off all the furniture with soft cloths, they water the
plants, they pick up any litter which may have ac-
cumulated, they learn the habit of really examining
a room to see if it is in order or not. One natural
result of this daily training in close observation of a
room is a much greater care in the use of it during
the day, a result the importance of which can be
certified by any mother who has to " pick up " after
a family of small children.

After the room is fresh and clean, the " order of
exercises " is very flexible, varying according to circumstances, the weather, the desire of the children.
They may perhaps sing a hymn together before dis-
persing to their different self-chosen exercises with
the apparatus. Sometimes the teacher gives them
some exercises in manners, showing them how to rise
gracefully and quietly from their little chairs, how to
say good-morning; how to give and receive politely

some object; how to carry things safely across the
room, etc., etc. Sometimes they all sit about the
teacher and have a talk with her, an exercise in ordinary well-bred conversation which is sadly needed by
our American children, who are seldom, at least as
young as this, trained to express themselves in any
but trivial requests, or, as in the kindergarten, in repeating stories. The teacher questions the children
about the happenings of their lives, about anything
of more general interest which they may have observed, or on any topic which excites a general interest
which they may have observed. Of course, because she
is a Montessori teacher she does as little of this talking
as possible herself, confining herself to brief remarks
which may draw out the children. Such conversation is of the greatest help to the fluency and cor-
rectness of speech and to an early enriching of the
vocabulary, all important factors in the release of
the child from the prison of his baby limitations.
The habit of listening while others talk acquired in
these general morning conversations is also of incalculable value, as is attested by the proverbial rarity
of the good listener even among adults.

Of course the main business of the day is the use
of the apparatus, the different Montessori exercises,
and these soon occupy the attention of all the children. With intervals of outdoor play in the courtyard garden, care of the plants there, the morning
progresses till the lunch hour, which has been described. After this, or indeed, whenever they feel

sleepy, the smaller children take their naps, and they
do not go home until five or six o'clock in the afternoon, having back of them a peaceful, harmonious
day, every instant of which has been actively, happily,
and profitably employed, and which has been full
from morning till night of goodwill and comrade-
ship.

From time to time it happens that a new brother
or sister is introduced into this big family, with its
régime of perfect freedom from unnecessary restraint. The behavior of children who are brought
into the school after the beginning of the school-
year is naturally extremely various, since they are
allowed then, as always, to express with perfect liberty their own individualities. Some join at once, of
their own accord, in one or another of the interesting
" games " they see being played by the other children
already initiated, and in half an hour are indis-
tinguishable from the older inhabitants of that little
world, drawing their fingers alternately over sandpaper and smooth wood to learn the difference between
" rough " and " smooth," or delightedly matching the
different-colored spools of silk. Others, naturally
shy ones, naturally reserved ones, those who have been
rendered suspicious by injudicious home treatment, or
those who have naturally slow mental machines, hold
aloof for a time. They are allowed to do this as long
as they please. They are welcomed once smilingly,
and then left to their own devices.

I remember, in the Via Giusti school, seeing for

several days in succession a tiny girl, not more than three, with wide, shy, fawn-eyes, sitting idle at a little table, in the middle of the morning, with all her wraps on. When I inquired the meaning of this very unusual sight, the Directress told me that, apparently, the child had something of the wild-animal terror of being caught in a trap, and had indicated, terrified, when her mother, on the first morning, tried to take off her cap and cloak, that she wished to be free at any moment to make her escape from these new and untried surroundings. So her wraps were not removed, she was allowed to sit near the door, which was kept ajar, and not a look or gesture from the Directress disturbed the reassuring isolation in which that baby, by slow degrees, found herself and learned her first lesson of the big world. I think she sat thus for three whole days, at first starting nervously if anyone chanced to approach her, with the painful, apprehensive glare of the constitutionally timid child, but little by little conquering herself.

One day she reached over shyly for a buttoning frame, left on the next table by a child who had wandered off to other joys. She sat with this some time, looking about suspiciously to see if some adult were meditating that condescending swoop of patronizing congratulation which is so offensive to the self-respecting pride of a naturally reserved personality. No one noticed her. Still glancing up with frequent suspicious starts, she began trying to insert the buttons in the buttonholes, and then, by degrees, lost

herself, forgot entirely the tragic self-consciousness
which had embittered her little life, and with a real
" Montessori face," a countenance of ardent, happy,
self-forgetting interest in overcoming obstacles, she
set definitely to work. After a time, finding that her
cape impeded her motions, she flung it off, taking
unconsciously the step into which, three days before,
only superior physical force could have coerced
her.

I watched her through the winter with much interest, her reticent, self-contained nature always mark-
ing her off from the other little ones more or less,
and I rejoiced to see that all the natural manifestations of her differing individuality were religiously
respected by the wise Directress. It was not long
before she was trotting freely about the room chang
ing her activities with lively delight, and looking on
with friendly, though never very intimate, interest at
the doings of the other children. But it was months
before she cared to join at all in enterprises undertaken in common by the majority of the pupils, the
rollicking file, for instance, which stamped about
lustily in time to the music. She watched them, half-
astonished, half-disapproving, wholly contented with
her own permitted aloofness, like a slim little grey-
hound watching the light-hearted, heavy-footed antics
of a litter of Newfoundland puppies. At least one
person who saw her thanked Heaven many times
that a kind Providence had saved her from well-meaning adult efforts to make her over according to the

Newfoundland pattern. Hers was a rare individuality, the integrity of which was being preserved entire for the future leavening of an all-too-uniform civilization. For although the Montessori school furnishes the best possible practical training for democracy, inasmuch as every child learns speedily first the joys of self-dependence and then the self-abnegating pleasure of serving others, it is also preparing the greatest possible amelioration of our present-day democracy, by counteracting that bad, but apparently not inevitable, tendency of democracy to a dead level of uniform and characterless mediocrity. The Casa dei Bambini proves in actual practice that even the best interests of the sacred majority do not demand that powerful and differing individualities be forced into a common mould, but only guided into the higher forms of their own natural activities.

This brief digression is an illustration of the way in which every thoughtful observer in a Montessori school falls from time to time into a brown study which takes him far afield from the busy babies before him. No greater tribute to the broadly human and universal foundation of the system could be presented than this inevitable tendency in visitors to see in the differing childish activities the unchaining of great natural forces for good which have been kept locked and padlocked by our inertia, our short-sightedness, our lack of confidence in human nature, and our deeprooted and unfounded prejudice about childhood, our instinctive, mistaken, harsh conviction that it will be industrious, law-abiding, and self-controlled only under pressure from the outside.

It must be admitted that there is one variety of child who is the mortal terror of Montessori teachers. This is not the violently insubordinate child, because his violence and insubordination at home only indicate a strong nature which requires nothing but proper activities to turn it to powerful and energetic life. No, what reduces a Montessori teacher to despair is a child like one I saw in a school for the children of the wealthy, a beautiful, exquisitely attired little fairy of four, whose lovely, healthful body had been cared for with the most scientific exactitude by trained nurses, governesses, and nurse-maids, and the very springs of whose natural initiative and invention seemed to have been broken by the debilitating ministrations of all those caretakers. It is significant that the teacher of this school admitted to me that she found her carefully-reared pupils generally more listless, more selfish, harder to reach, and harder to stimulate than poor children; but the least prosperous of us need not think that because we cannot afford nurse-maids our children will fare better than those of millionaires, for one too devoted mother can equal a regiment of servants in crushing out a child's initiative, his natural desire for self-dependence, his self-respect, and his natural instinct for self-education.

The great point of vantage of a Montessori school

over an ordinary school in dealing with these morally starved children of too prosperous parents, is that it catches them younger, before the pernicious habit of passive dependence has continued long enough entirely to wreck their natural instincts. Beside the beautiful child of four with the sapped and weakened willpower mentioned above, was an equally beautiful, exquisitely dressed little tot of just three, whose glowing face of happy energy provided the most welcome contrast to the saddening mental torpor of the older child, who, though naturally in every way a normal little girl, stood hopelessly apathetic before all the fascinating lures to her invention which the Montessori apparatus spread before her. The little girl of three, without a word from the teacher, regulated for herself a busy, profitable, happy, purposeful life, getting out one piece of apparatus after another, " playing " with it until her fresh interest was gone, putting it away, and falling with equal ardor upon something else. The older child regarded her with the curious passive wonder of a Hindu when he sees us Occidentals getting our fun out of dancing and engaging in various active sports ourselves instead of reclining upon pillows to watch other people paid thus to exert themselves. She was given a choice of geometric insets, and provided with colored pencils and a big sheet of paper, baits which not even an idiot child can resist, and, sitting uninventive before this delightful array, remarked with a polite indifference that she was used to having people draw pictures for her. The poor child had acquired the habit of having somebody else do even her playing.

In the face of this melancholy sight, I was comforted by the teacher's hopeful assurance that the child had made some advance since the beginning of the school, and showed some signs that intellectual activity was awakening naturally under the wellnigh irresistible stimulus of the Montessori apparatus.

One exception to the general truth that the children in a Montessori school do not take concerted action is in the " lesson of silence." This is often mentioned in accounts of the Casa dei Bambini, but it is so important that it may perhaps be here described again. It originated as a lesson for one of the senses, hearing, but though it undoubtedly is an excellent exercise for the ears it has a moral effect which is more important. It is certainly to visitors one of the most impressive of all the impressive sights to be seen in the Children's Home.

One may be moving about between the groups of busy children, or sitting watching their lively animation or listening to the cheerful hum of their voices, when one feels a curious change in the atmosphere like the hush which falls on a forest when the sun suddenly goes behind a cloud. If it is the first time one has seen this " lesson," the effect is startling. A quick glance around shows that the children have stopped playing as well as talking, and are sitting motionless at their tables, their eyes on the black-

board where in large letters is written " Silenzio "
(Silence). Even the little ones who cannot read, follow the example of the older ones, and not only sit
motionless, but look fixedly at the magic word. The
Directress is visible now, standing by the blackboard
in an attitude and with an expression of tranquillity
which is as calming to see as the meditative impassiv-
ity of a Buddhist priest. The silence becomes more
and more intense. To untrained ears it seems absolute, but an occasional faint gesture or warning
smile from the Directress shows that a little hand has
moved almost but not quite inaudibly, or a chair
has creaked.

At first the children smile in answer, but soon,
under the hypnotic peace of the hush which lasts minute after minute, even this silent interchange of loving admonition and response ceases. It is now evident from the children's trance-like immobility that
they no longer need to make an effort to be motionless. They sit quiet, rapt in a vague, brooding reverie,
their busy brains lulled into repose, their very souls
looking out from their wide, vacant eyes. This expression of utter peace, which I never before saw on a
child's face except in sleep, has in it something profoundly touching. In that matter-of-fact, modern
schoolroom, as solemnly as in shadowy cathedral
aisles, falls for an instant a veil of contemplation,
between the human soul and the external realities of
the world.

And then a real veil of twilight falls to intensify

the effect. The Directress goes quietly about from window to window, closing the shutters. In the ensuing twilight, the children bow their heads on their clasped hands in the attitude of prayer. The Directress steps through the door into the next room and a slow voice, faint and clear, comes floating back, calling a child's name.

" El...e...na! "

A child lifts her head, opens her eyes, rises as silently as a little spirit, and with a glowing face of exaltation, tiptoes out of the room, flinging herself joyously into the waiting arms.

The summons comes again, " Vit...to...ri...o! "

A little boy lifts his head from his desk, showing a face of sweet, sober content at being called, and goes silently across the big room, taking his place by the side of the Directress. And so it goes until perhaps fifteen children are clustered happily about the teacher. Then, as informally and naturally as it began, the " game " is over. The teacher comes back into the room with her usual quiet, firm step; light pours in at the windows; the mystic word is erased from the blackboard. The visitor is astonished to see that only six or seven minutes have passed since the beginning of this new experience. The children smile at each other, and begin to play again, perhaps a little more quietly than before, perhaps more gently, certainly with the shining eyes of devout believers who have blessedly lost themselves in an instant of rapt and self-forgetting devotion.

And, in a sense, they too have been to church. This modern scientific Roman woman-doctor, who probably never heard of William Penn, has rediscovered the mystic joys of his sect, and has appropriated to her system one of the most beneficial elements of the Quaker Meeting.

Before seeing this "lesson of silence" one does not realize that there is a lack in the world of the Casa dei Bambini. After seeing it one feels instantly that it is an essential element, this brief period of perfect repose from the mental activity which, though unstimulated, is practically incessant; this brief excursion away from all the restless, shifting, rapid things of the world into the region of peace and calm and immobility. And yet who of us, without seeing this in actual practice, would ever have dreamed that little children would care for such an exercise, would submit to it for an instant, much less throw themselves into it with all the ardor of little Yogis, and emerge from it sweeter, more obedient, calmed, and gentler as from a tranquilizing prayer? Sometimes, once in a day is not enough for them, and later they ask of their own accord to have this experience repeated. Their pleasure in it is inexpressible. The expression which comes over their little faces when, in the midst of their busy play, they feel the first hush fall about them is something never to be forgotten.

It makes one feel a sort of envy of these children who are so much better understood than we were at their age. And the fact that our own hearts are somehow calmed and refreshed by this bath of silent peace makes one wonder if we are not all of us still children enough to benefit by many of the habits of life taught there, to profit by the adaptation to our adult existence of some of the principles underlying this scheme of education for babies.

CHAPTER IV

SOMETHING ABOUT THE APPARATUS AND ABOUT THE THEORY UNDERLYING IT

AS I look at the title of this chapter before setting to work on it, the sight of the word " Theory " makes me apprehensively aware that I am stepping down into very deep water without any great confidence in my powers as a swimmer. But I recall again the reflection which has buoyed me up more than once in the composition of these unscientific impressions, namely that I am addressing an audience no more scientific than I am, an audience of ordinary, fairly well educated American parents. Furthermore I am convinced that my book can do no more valuable service than if by the tentative incompleteness of its account it drives every reader to the study of the system in Dr. Montessori's own carefully written treatise.

It is always, I believe, essential to an understanding of any educational system to comprehend first of all the underlying principle before going on to its adaptation to actual conditions. This adaptation naturally varies as the actual conditions vary, and should change in many details if it is to embody faithfully, under differing conditions, the fundamental principle. But the master idea in every system is unvarying,

eternal, and it should be stated, studied, and grasped,
before any effort is made to learn the details of its
practical application. A statement of this fundamental principle will be found in different phrasings,
several times in the course of this book, because it is
essential not only to learn it once, but to bear it constantly in mind. *Any attempt to use the Montessori
apparatus or system by anyone who does not fully
grasp or is not wholly in sympathy with its bed-
rock idea, results inevitably in a grotesque, tragic
caricature of the method,* such a farcical spectacle as
we now see the attempt to Christianize people by
forcible baptism to have been.

The central idea of the Montessori system, on
which every smallest bit of apparatus, every detail
of technic rests solidly, is a full recognition of the
fact that no human being can be educated by anyone
else. He must do it himself or it is never done. And
this is as true at the age of three as at the age of
thirty; even truer, for the man of thirty is at least
as physically strong as any self-proposed mentor is
apt to be, and can fight for his own right to chew
and digest his own intellectual food.

It can be readily seen how this dominating idea
changes completely the old-established conditions in
the schoolroom, turning the high light from the
teacher to the pupil. Since the child can really be
taught nothing by the teacher, since he himself must
do every scrap of his own learning, it is upon the
child that our attention centers. The teacher should

be the all-wise observer of his natural activity, giving
him such occasional quick, light-handed guidance as
he may for a moment need, providing for him in the
shape of the ingenious Montessori apparatus stimuli
for his intellectual life and materials which enable him
to correct his own mistakes; but, by no means, as
has been our old-time notion, taking his hand in hers
and leading him constantly along a fixed path, which
she or her pedagogical superiors have laid out beforehand, and into which every childish foot must be
either coaxed or coerced.

We have admitted the entire validity of this theory
in physical life. We no longer send our children for
their outdoor exercise bidding them walk along the
street, holding to Nurse's hand like little ladies and
gentlemen. If we can possibly manage it we turn
them loose with a sandpile, a jumping-rope, hoops,
balls, bats, and other such stimuli to their natural
instinct for vigorous body-developing exercise. And
we have a " supervisor " in our public playgrounds
only to see that children are rightly started in their
use of the different games, not at all to play every
game with them. We do this nowadays because we
have learned that little children are so devoted to
those exercises which tend to increase their bodily
strength that they need no urging to engage in them.
The Montessori child, analogously, is allowed and
encouraged to let go the hand of his mental nurse, to
walk and run about on his own feet, and an almost
endless variety of stimuli to his natural instinct for

vigorous mind-developing, intellectual exercise is placed within his reach.

The teacher, under this system, is the scientific, observing supervisor of this mental " playground " where the children acquire intellectual vigor, independence, and initiative as spontaneously, joyfully, and tirelessly as they acquire physical independence and vigor as a by-product of physical play. We have long realized that children do not need to be driven by force, or even persuaded, to take the amount of exercise necessary to develop their growing bodies. Indeed the difficulty has been to keep them from doing it so continuously as to interfere with our sedentary adult occupations and tastes. We have learned that all we need to do is to provide the jumping-rope and then leave the child alone with other children. The most passionately inspired pedagogue can never learn to skip rope for a child, any more than in after years he can ever learn the conjugation of a single irregular verb for a pupil. The learner must do his own learning, and, this granted, it follows naturally that the less he is interfered with by arbitrary restraint and vexatious, unnecessary rules, the more quickly and easily he will learn. An observation of the typical, joyfully busy child in a Casa dei Bambini furnishes more than sufficient proof that he enjoys acquiring mental as well as physical agility and strength, and asks nothing better than a fair and unhindered chance at this undertaking.

But even when this deep-laid foundation principle

of self-education has been grasped, all is not plain sailing for the adventurer on the Montessori ocean. A set of theories relating to such complicated organisms as human beings, cannot in the nature of things be of primer-like simplicity. For my own convenience I very soon made two main divisions of the different branches on which the Montessori system is developed out of its central main idea. One division, the practical, is made up of theories based on acute, scientific knowledge of the child's body, his muscles, brain, and nerves, such as only a doctor and a physiological psychologist combined can have. The second division is made up of theories based on the spiritual nature of man, as disclosed by the study of history, by unbiased direct observation of present-day society, and by that divining fervor of enthusiastic reverence for the element of perfectibility in human nature which has always characterized founders of new religions.

This chapter is to be devoted to the narration of what a person, neither a doctor nor a physiological psychologist, was able to understand of the first division.

I think the first point which struck me especially was the insistence on the fact that very little children have no greater natural interest than in learning how to do something with their bodies. We all know how much more fascinating a place our kitchens seem to be for our little children than our drawing-rooms. I have heard this inevitable gravitation towards those back regions of the house accounted for on the theory the " children seem to like servants better than other people. There seems to be some sort of natural affinity between a child and a cook." One morning spent in the Casa dei Bambini showed me the true reason. Children like cooks and chamber-maids better than callers in the parlor, because servants are always doing something imitable; and they like kitchens and pantries better than drawing-rooms because the drawing-room is a museum full of objects, interesting it is true, but inclosed in the padlocked glass-case of the command, " Now, don't touch!" while the kitchen is a veritable treasure-house of Montessori apparatus.

The three-year-old child who, eluding pursuit from the front of the house, sits down on the kitchen floor with a collection of cookie-cutters of different shapes in his lap, and amuses himself by running his fingers around their edges, is engaged in a true " stereognostic exercise " as it is alarmingly dubbed in scientific nomenclature. If there is a closet of pots and pans, and he has time before he is dragged off to clean clothes and the vacuity of adult-invented toys, to fit the right covers to the pots and see which pan goes inside which, he has gone through a " sensory exercise for developing his sense of dimension." If he is struck by the fact that the package of oatmeal, although so large, weighs less than the smaller bag of salt, he has been initiated into a " baric exercise "; while if there are some needles of ice left on the floor by a careless iceman, with these and a permitted dabbling in warm dishwater, he unconsciously invents for himself a " thermic exercise." If the cook is indulgent or too busy to notice, there may be added to these interests the creative rapture to be evolved from a lump of dough, or a fumbling attempt to fathom the mysterious inwardness of a Dover eggbeater.

I have heard it said of the Montessori method that a system of education accomplished with such simple everyday means could scarcely claim that it is either anything new or the discovery of any one person. It seems to me that is about like denying any novelty to the discovery that pure air will cure consumption. The pure air has always been there, consumptives have had nothing to do but to breathe it to get well, but the doctors who first drove that fact into our impervious heads deserve some credit and can certainly claim that they were innovators with their descent upon the stuffy sickrooms and their command to open the windows.

Children from time immemorial have always done their best, struggling bravely against the tyranny of adult good intentions, to educate themselves by training their senses in all sorts of sense exercise. They have always been (generations of exasperated mothers can bear witness to it!) " possessed " to touch and handle all objects about them. What Dr. Montessori has done is to appear suddenly, like the window-breaking doctors, and to cry to us, " Let them do it! " Or rather, to suggest something better for them to touch and handle since it is neither necessary nor desirable that one's three-year-old should perfect his sense of form either on one's cherished Sèvres vase or on a more or less greasy cooking utensil. Nor has he that perverse fondness for the grease of the kettle, or that wicked joy in the destruction of valuable bric-à-brac which our muddle-headed observation has led us to attribute to him. Those are merely fortuitous, and for him negligible, accompaniments to the process of learning how to distinguish accurately different forms. Dr. Montessori assures us, and proves her assertion, that his sole interest is in the varying shapes of the utensils he handles, and that if he is given cleaner, lighter articles with more interesting shapes, he requires no urging to turn to them from his greasy and heavy pots and pans.

Bearing in mind, therefore, the humble and familiar relatives of the Montessori apparatus to be found in our own kitchens and dining-rooms, let us look at it a little more in detail.

The buttoning-frames have been described (page 13). One's invention can vary them nearly to infinity. In the Casa dei Bambini there are these frames arranged for buttons and buttonholes, for hooks and eyes, for lacings, patent snap-fasteners, ribbon-ends to tie, etc., etc. The aim of this exercise is so apparent that it is scarcely necessary to mention it, except for the constant temptation of a child-lover before the Montessori apparatus to see in it only the most enchanting diversion for a child, which amuses him, though so simply, far more than the most elaborate of mechanical toys. But, and here is where our wool-gathering wits must learn a lesson from purposeful forethought: we should never forget that *there is no smallest item in the Montessori training which is intended merely to amuse the child.* He is given these buttoning-frames not because they fascinate him and keep him out of mischief, but because they help him to learn to handle, more rapidly than he otherwise would, the various devices by which his clothes and shoes are held together, on his little body. As for the profound and vitally important reason why he should be taught and allowed as soon as possible to dress himself, that will be treated in the discussion of the philosophical side of this baby-training (page 129 ff.).

It is apparent, of course, that the blindfolded child who was identifying the pieces of different fabrics was training his sense of touch. The sight of this exercise reminds the average person with a start of surprise that he too was born with a sense of touch which might have been cultivated if anyone had thought of it; for most of us, by the enormity of our neglect of our five senses, reduce them, for all practical purposes to two, sight and hearing, and distrust any information which comes to us by other means. Our complacency under this self-imposed deprivation is astonishing. It is as if a man should wear a patch over one eye because he is able to see with one and thinks it not worth while to use two.

EXERCISES IN PRACTICAL LIFE.

BUILDING "THE TOWER."

Now, it is apparent that our five senses are our only means of conveying information to our brains about the external world which surrounds us, and it is equally apparent that to act wisely and surely in the world, the brain has need of the fullest and most accurate information possible. Hence it is a foregone conclusion, once we think of it at all, that the education of all the senses of a child to rapidity, agility, and exactitude is of great importance, not at all for the sake of the information acquired at the time by the child, but for the sake of the five, finely accurate instruments which this education puts under his control. The child who was identifying the different fabrics was blindfolded to help him concentrate his sense of touch on the problem and not aid this sense or mislead it, as we often do, with his sight.

It may be well here to set down a few facts about the relative positions of the senses of touch and of sight, facts which are not known to many of us, and the importance of which is not realized by many who happen to know them. Everyone knows, to begin with, that a new-born baby's eyes, while physically perfect, are practically useless, and that the ability to see with them accurately comes very gradually. It seems that it comes much more gradually than the people usually in charge of little children have ever known, and that, roughly speaking, up to the age of six, children need to have their vision reinforced by touch if, without great mental fatigue, they are to get an accurate conception of the objects about them.

It appears furthermore that, as if in compensa-
tion for this slow development of vision, the sense of
touch is extraordinarily developed in young children.
In short, that the natural way for little ones to
learn about things is to touch them.   Dr. Montessori found that the finger-tips of little children
are extremely sensitive, and she claims that there is
no necessity, granted proper training, why this valuable faculty, only retained by most adults in the
event of blindness, should be lost so completely in
later life.

Now it is plain to be seen that we adults, with our
fixed habit of learning about things from looking at
them, have, in neglecting this means of approach to
the child-brain, been losing a golden opportunity.
If children learn more quickly and with less fatigue
through their fingers than through their eyes, why
not take advantage of this peculiarity—a peculiarity
which extends even more vividly to child-memory, for
it is established beyond question that a little child
can remember the " feel " of a given object much
more accurately and quickly than the look of it.   It
is easy to understand, once this explanation is given,
the great stress that is laid, in Montessori training, on
the different exercises for developing and utilizing
the sense of touch.

One of the first things a child just admitted to a Casa
dei Bambini is taught is to keep his hands scrupu-
lously clean, because we can " touch things better "
with clean finger-tips than with dirty ones.   And, of

course, he is allowed to take the responsibility of keeping his own hands clean, and encouraged to do it by the presence of the little dainty washstands, just the right height for him, supplied with bowl, pitcher, etc., just the right size for him to handle. The joy of the children in these simple little washstands, and their deft, delighted, frequent use of them is a reproach to us for not furnishing such an easily secured amelioration in the life of every one of our babies.

The education of the sense of touch, like all the Montessori exercises for the senses, begins with a few simple and strongly contrasting sensations and proceeds little by little, to many only very slightly differing sensations, following the growth of the child's ability to differentiate. The child with clean finger-tips begins, therefore, with the first broad distinction between rough and smooth. He is taught to pass his finger-tips lightly, first over a piece of sand-paper, and then over a piece of smoothly polished wood, or glossy enameled paper, and is told briefly, literally in two words, the two names of those two abstract qualities.

Here, in passing, with the first mention of this sort of exercise, it should be stated that the children are taught to make these movements of the hand and all others like them *always* from left to right, so that a muscular habit will be established which will aid them greatly later when they come to " feel " their letters, which are, of course, always written from left to right.

The children are encouraged to keep their eyes
closed while they are " touching " things, because
they can concentrate their attention in this way.
And here another general observation should be
made: that in the Montessori language " touching "
does not mean the brief haphazard contact of hand
with object which we usually mean, but a systematic
examination of an object by the finger-tips such as a
blind person might make.

After the first broad distinction is learned between
rough and smooth, there are then to be conquered all
the intervening shades and refinements of those qualities. The children take the greatest delight in these
exercises and almost at once begin to invent new ones
for themselves, " feeling " whatever materials are
near them and giving them their proper names, or
asking what their names are. It is as if their little
minds were suddenly opened, as our dully perceptive
adult minds seldom are, to the infinite variety of sur-
faces in the world. They notice the materials of
their own dresses, the stuffs used in upholstering furniture, curtains, dress fabrics, wood, smooth and
rough, steel, glass, etc., etc., with exquisitely fairy-
light strokes of their sensitive little finger-tips,
which seem almost visibly to grow more discriminating.

The " technical apparatus " for continuing this
training is varied, but always simple. A collection of
slips of sandpaper of varying roughness to be placed
in order from fine to coarse by the child (blindfolded

or not, as he seems to prefer) ; other collections of
bits of fabrics of all sorts to be identified by touch
only ; of slips of cardboard, enameled or rough ;
blotting-paper, writing-paper, newspaper, etc., etc. ;
of objects of different shapes, cubes, pyramids, balls,
cylinders, etc., for the blindfolded child to identify ;
later on of very small objects like seeds of different
shapes or sizes ; finally, of any objects which the
child knows by sight, his playthings, articles around
the house, to be recognized by his touch only.

There is one result on the child's character of this
sort of exercise which Dr. Montessori does not spe-
cifically mention but which has struck me forcibly in
practical experimentation with it.   I have found that
little hands and fingers trained by these fascinating
" games " to light, attentive, discriminating, and unhurried handling of objects, lose very quickly that
instinctive childish, violent but very uncertain clutch
at things, which has been for so many generations
the cause of so much devastation in the nursery.
Little tots of four, trained in this way, can be trusted
with glassware and other breakable objects, which
would go down to certain destruction in the fitfully
governed hands of the average undisciplined child of
twelve.   In other words the child of four has fitted
himself by means of a highly enjoyable process to be,
in one more respect, an independent, self-respecting,
trustworthy citizen of his world.

Of course all these different exercises are much
more entertaining when, like other fun-producing

"games," they are "played" with a crowd of other children. When one child of a group is blindfolded, and as our American children say "It," while the others sit about, watching his identification of more and more difficult objects, ready, all of them, for a shout of applause at a success, or at a failure for an instant laughing pounce on the coveted blindfold and application of it to the child next in order, of course there is much more jolly laughter, the interest is keener, and the attention more concentrated by the contact with other wits, than can be the case with a single child, even with an audience of the most sympathetic mother or aunt. There is absolutely no adequate substitute for the beneficial action and reaction of children upon one another such as form such a considerable part of the Montessori training in a Casa dei Bambini. On the other hand, those of us who live, as we almost all do, far from any variety of a Montessori school, can, with the exercise of our ingenuity and mother-wit, arrange a great number of more or less adequate temporary expedients. A large number of the Montessori devices, if they were not called "sensory exercises," would be recognized as merely fascinating new games for children. What is blind-man's buff but a "sensory exercise for training the ear," since what the person who is "It" does is to try to catch the slight movements made by the other players accurately enough to pursue and capture them? Children have another game called, for some mysterious reason of

childhood, " Still pond, no more moving! " a variety
of blind-man's buff, which trains still more finely the
sense of hearing, since the players are required to
stand perfectly still, and the one who is " It " must
detect their presence by such almost imperceptible
sounds as their breathing, or the rustling caused by
an involuntary movement. If Montessori herself
had invented this game, it could not be more perfectly devised for bodily control. Children who
wriggle about in ordinary circumstances without the
slightest capacity to control their bodies, even in response to the sternest adult commands for quiet, will
stand in some strained position without moving a
finger, their concentration so intense that even their
breathing is light and inaudible. We must all have
seen children happily playing such games ; many of
us have spent hours and hours of our childhood over
them ; Froebel used them and others like them plenti-
fully in his system ; there are all sorts of more or less
hit-or-miss imitations of them being constructed by
modern child-tamers ; but no one before this Italian
woman-doctor ever analyzed them so that we plain
unprofessional people could fully grasp their fascination for us ; ever told us that children like them
because they afford an opportunity to practise self-
control, and that similar games based on the same
idea that it is " fun " to exercise one's different
senses in company or in competition with one's youthful contemporaries, would be just as entertaining as
these self-invented games, handed down for untold

generations from one set of children to another. All the varieties of blindfold sensory exercises are variations on the theme of blind-man's buff, which is so perennially interesting to all children. Any small group of young children, two or three little neighbors come in to play, will with a little guidance at first readily " play " any of the " tactile exercises " described above (pages 60, 61) for hours on end, instead of wrangling about the rocking-horse—a toy invented for solitary or semi-solitary consumption. Any group of children, collected anywhere for ever so short a time, can be converted into a half-hour's Montessori school, though as a rule the younger they are the better material they are, since they have not fallen into bad mental habits.

The various exercises or " games " for exercising the sense of touch, although not described here in all the detail of their elaboration in the Casa dei Bambini, can be elaborated from these suggestions as one's own, or what is more likely, the children's inventiveness may make possible.

The definite education of taste and smell has not been very much developed by Dr. Montessori, although simple exercises have been successfully devised, such as dropping on the tongue tiny particles of substances, sweet, sour, salt, bitter, etc., having the child rinse his mouth out carefully between each test. Similar exercises with different-smelling substances can be undertaken with blindfolded children, asking them to guess what they are smelling. Dr. Montes-

sori lays no great stress on this, however, as the sense
of smell with children is not highly developed.

Practice in judging weight is given by the use of
pieces of wood of the same size but of different
weights, chestnut contrasted with oak, poplar-wood
with maple, etc., etc., the child learning by slightly
lifting them up and down on the palm of his hand.
Later on this can be varied by the use of any objects
of about the same size but of different weights, and
later still by single objects of weights dispropor-
tionate to their size, such as a bit of lead or a small
pillow.

The difference between these carefully devised exercises and the haphazard, almost unconscious comparison by the child in the kitchen of the bag of salt
and the box of oatmeal, is a very good example of
the way in which Dr. Montessori has systematized
and ordered, graded and arranged the exercises which
every child instinctively craves. The average mother,
with leisure to devote to her much-loved child, calls
him away from the pantry-shelf where he may upset
the oatmeal box or spill the salt, thus " getting into
mischief," and leads him, with mistaken affection,
back to his toy animals. The luckier child of a
poorer, busier, or more indifferent mother is allowed
to "mess around" in the kitchen until he makes himself too intolerable a nuisance. He goes through in
this way many valuable sense exercises, but he wastes
a great deal of his time in misdirected and futile
effort, and does, as a matter of fact, make a great

deal of trouble for his elders which is not at all a
necessary accompaniment to his own life, liberty, or
pursuit of information.

Dr. Montessori has neither led the child away from
his instinctively chosen occupations, nor left him in
the state of anarchic chaos resulting from his natural inability to choose, among the bewildering variety
of objects in the world, those which are best suited
for his self-development. She has, so to speak, taken
out into the kitchen, beside the child, busy with his
self-chosen amusements, her highly trained brain,
stored with pertinent scientific information, and she
has looked at him long and hard. As a result she is
able to show us, what our own blurred observation
never would have distinguished, just which elements,
in the heterogeneous mass of his naturally preferred
toys, are the elements towards which the tendrils of
his rapidly-growing intellectual and muscular organism are reaching.

CHAPTER V

DESCRIPTION OF THE REST OF THE APPA-
RATUS AND THE METHOD FOR WRITING
AND READING

THE carefully graded advance, from the simpler to the harder exercises, which is so essential a part of the correct use of the Montessori, as of all other educational apparatus, seems to most mothers contemplating the use of the system, a very difficult feature. " How am I to know? " they ask. " Which exercise is the best one to offer a child to begin with, how can I tell when he has sufficiently mastered that so that another is needed, and how shall I select the right one to go on with? "

Perhaps the first answer to make to these questions is the one which so often successfully solves Montessori problems: " Have a little more trust in your child's natural instincts. Don't think that a single mistake on your part will be fatal. It will not hurt him if you happen to suggest the wrong thing, if you do not insist on it, for, left freely to himself, he will not pay the least attention to anything that is not suitable for him. Give him opportunity for perfectly free action, and then *watch him carefully*."

If he shows a lively spontaneous interest in a Montessori problem, and devotes himself to solving it,

you may be sure that you have hit upon something
which suits his degree of development. If he goes
through with it rather easily and, perhaps, listlessly,
and needs your reminder to keep his attention on it,
in all probability it is too easy; he has outgrown it,
he no longer cares to occupy himself with it, just as
you no longer care to jump rope, though that may
have been a passion with you at the age of eight.

If, on the other hand, he seems distressed at the
difficulties before him, and calls repeatedly for help
and explanation, one of three conditions is present.
Either the exercise is too hard for him, or he has acquired already the bad habit of dependence on others,
in both of which cases he needs an easier exercise; or,
lastly, he has simply had enough formal " sensory exercises " for a while. It is the most mistaken notion about the Montessori Children's Home to conceive that the children are occupied from morning
till night over the apparatus of her formal instruction. They use it exactly as long, or as often, or as
seldom, as they please, just as a child in an ordinary
nursery uses his ordinary toys. It must be kept constantly in mind that the wonderful successes attained
by the Montessori schools in Rome cannot be repeated
by the mere repetition of sensory exercises, thrust
spasmodically into the midst of another system, or
lack of system, in child-training. The Italian children of five or six, who have had two or three years
of Montessori discipline, and who are such marvels
of sweet, reasonable self-control, who govern their

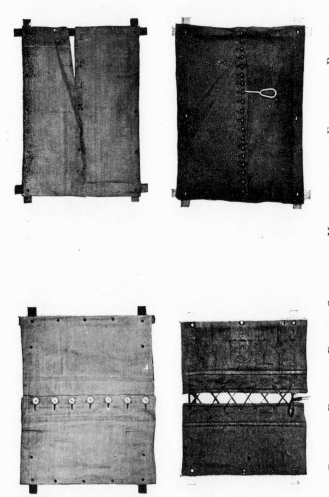

BUTTONING-FRAMES TO DEVELOP CO-ORDINATED MOVEMENTS OF THE FINGERS AND PREPARE THE CHILDREN FOR EXERCISES OF PRACTICAL LIFE.

own lives so sanely, who have accomplished such astonishing feats in reading and writing, are the results of many other factors besides buttoning-frames and geometric insets, important as these are.

Perhaps the most vital of these other factors is the sense of responsibility, genuine responsibility, not the make-believe kind, with which we are too often apt to put off our children when they first show their touchingly generous impulse to share some of the burdens of our lives. For instance, to take a rather extreme instance, but one which we must all have seen, a child in an ordinary home is allowed to pick up a bit of waste-paper on the floor, after having had his attention called to it, and is told to throw it in the waste-paper basket. This action of mechanical obedience, suitable only for a child under two years of age, is then praised insincerely to the child's face as an instance of " how *much* help he is to Mother! "

The Montessori child is trained, through his feeling of responsibility for the neatness and order of his schoolroom, to notice litter on the floor, just as any housekeeper does, without needing to have her attention called to it. It is her floor and her business to keep it clean. And this feeling of responsibility is fostered and allowed every opportunity to grow strong, by the sincere conviction of the Montessori teacher that it is more important for the child to feel it, than for the floor to be cleaned with adult speed. As a result of this long patience on the part of the Directress, a child who has been under her care for a couple of years, will (to go on with our chosen instance) pick up litter from the floor and dispose of it, as automatically as the mistress of the house herself, and with as little need for the goad either of upbraiding for neglect, or praise incommensurate with the trivial service. This is an attitude in marked contrast to that of many of our daughters who often attain high-school age without acquiring this feeling, apparently perfectly possible to inculcate if the process is begun early enough, of loyal solidarity with the interests of the household.

With this caution that a Montessori life for a little child does not in the least mean his incessant occupation with formal sensory exercises, let us again take up the description and use of the apparatus.

The first thing which is given a child is usually either one of the buttoning-frames (shown in the illustration facing page 68), or what are called the " solid geometric insets." This latter game with the formidable name is illustrated opposite this page, where it is seen to resemble the set of weights kept beside their scales by old-fashioned druggists. No other Montessori exercise is more universally popular with the littlest ones who enter the Children's Home, and few others hold their attention so long. This combines training for both sight and touch, since, as an aid to his vision, the child is taught to run his finger-tips around the cylinder which he is trying to fit in, and then around the edges of the holes. His finger-tips recognize the similarity of

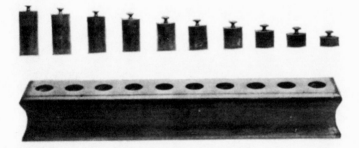

SOLID GEOMETRICAL INSETS.

size before his eyes do. This piece of apparatus is, of course, entirely self-corrective, and needs no supervision. When it becomes easy for a child quickly to get all the cylinders into the right holes, he has probably had enough of this exercise, although his interest in it may recur from time to time, during many weeks.

One of the exercises which it is usual to offer him next is the construction of the Tower. This game could be played (and often is) with the nest of hollow blocks which nearly every child owns, and it consists of building a pyramid with them, the biggest at the bottom, the next smaller on this, and so on to the apex made by the tiniest one. This is to learn the difference between big and small; and as the child progresses in exactitude of vision, the game can be varied by piling the blocks in confusion at one side of the room and constructing the pyramid, a piece at a time, at some distance away. This means that when the child leaves his pyramid to go and get the block needed next, he must " carry the size in his eye " as the phrase runs, and pick out the block next smaller by an effort of his visual memory.

The difference between long and short is taught by means of ten squared rods of equal thickness, but regularly varying length, the shortest one being just one-tenth as long as the longest. The so-called Long Stair (illustration facing page 74) is constructed by the child with these. This is perhaps the most difficult game among those by which dimensions are taught, and a good many mistakes are to be anticipated. The material is again quite self-corrective, however, and little by little, with occasional silent or brief reminders from the adult onlooker, the child learns first to correct his own mistakes, and then not to make them. Thickness and thinness are studied with ten solids, brick-like in shape, all of the same length, but of regularly varying thickness, the thinnest one being one-tenth as thick as the biggest one. With these the child constructs the Big Stair (illustration facing page 74). Later on (considerably later), when the child begins to learn his numbers, these " stairs " are used to help him. The large numbers cuts out of sandpaper and pasted on smooth cardboard, are placed by the child beside the right number of red and blue sections on each rod of the Long Stair.

After the construction of the Long and Big Stair the child is usually ready for the exercises with different fabrics to develop his sense of touch, and for the first beginning of the exercises leading to writing; especially the strips of sandpaper pasted upon smooth wood used to teach the difference between rough and smooth. At the same time with these exercises, begin the first ones with color which consist of simply matching spools of identical color, two by two.

When these simple exercises of the tactile sense have been mastered, the child is allowed to attempt the more difficult undertaking of recognizing all the

minute gradations between smoooth and rough, between dark blue and light blue, etc., etc.

The training of the eye to discriminate between
minute differences in shades, is carried on steadily in
a series of exercises which result in an accuracy of
vision in this regard which puts most of us adults to
shame. These color-games are played with silk
wound around flat cards, like those on which we often
buy our darning-cotton. There are eight main colors, and under each color eight shades, ranging from
dark to light. The number of games which can be
played with these is only limited by the ingenuity of
the Directress or mother, and, although most of
them are played more easily with a number of children together, many are quite available for the solitary " only child at home." He can amuse himself by
arranging his sixty-four bobbins in the correct order
of their colors, or he can later, as in the pyramid-
making game, pile them all on one side of the room,
and make his graduated line at a distance, " holding
the color " in his mind as he crosses the room, a feat
which almost no untrained adult can accomplish; although it is surprising what results can be obtained
any time in life by conscious, definite effort to train
one of the senses. There is nothing miraculous in
the results obtained in the Casa dei Bambini. They
are the simple, natural consequence of definite, direct
training, which is so seldom given. The remarkable
improvement in general acuteness of his vision after
training his eyes to follow the flight of bees, has been

picturesquely and vigorously recorded by John Burroughs; and all of us know how many more chestnuts we can see and pick up in a given time, after a few hours' concentration on this exercise, than when we first began to look for them in the grass.

The color-games played by a number of children together with the different-colored spools are various, but resemble more or less the old-fashioned game of authors. One of them is played thus. Eight children choose each the name of a color. Then the sixty-four spools are poured out in confusion on the table around which the children sit. One of them (the eldest or one chosen by lot) begins to deal out to the others in turn. That is, the one on his right asking for red, the dealer must quickly choose a spool of the right color and hand it to his neighbor. Then the child beyond asks for blue, and so it goes until the dealer makes a mistake. When he does, the deal goes to the child next him. After every child has before him in a mixed pile the eight shades of his chosen color, they all set to work as fast as they can to see who can soonest arrange them in the right chromatic order. The child who does this first has " won " the game, and is the one who deals first in the next game. Children of about the same age and ability repeat this game with the monotonously eternal vivid interest which characterizes an old-established quartet of whist-players, and they attain, by means of it and similar games with the color spools, a control of their eyes which is a marvel and which must forever add

THE BROAD STAIR.

THE LONG STAIR.

to the accuracy of their impressions about the world. When a generation of children trained in this manner has grown up, landscape painters will no longer be able to complain, as they do now, that they are working for a purblind public.

We are now approaching at last the extremely important and hitherto undescribed " geometric insets," whose mysterious name has piqued the curiosity of more than one casual and hasty reader of accounts of the Montessori system. A look at the pictures of these shows them to be as simple as all the rest of Dr. Montessori's expedients. Anyone who was ever touched by the picture-puzzle craze, or who in his childhood felt the fascination of dissected maps, needs no explanation of the pleasure taken by little children of four and five in fitting these queer-shaped bits of wood into their corresponding sockets, the square piece into the square socket, the triangle into the three-cornered hole, the four-leafed clover shape into the four-lobed recess. There can be no better description of the way in which a child is initiated into the use of this piece of apparatus than the one written by Miss Tozier for *McClure's Magazine*:

" A small boy of the mature age of four, who has been sitting plunged either in sleep or meditation, now starts up from his chair and wanders across to his directress for advice. He wants something to amuse him. She takes him to the cupboard, throws in a timely suggestion, and he strolls back to his table with a smile. He has chosen half a dozen or more thin, square tablets of wood and a strip of navy-blue cloth. He begins by spreading down the cloth, then he puts his blocks on it in two rows. They are of highly-varnished wood, light blue, with geometrical figures of navy-blue in the centre; there is a triangle, a circle, a rectangle, an oval, a square, an octagon. The teacher, who has followed him, stands on the other side of the table. She runs two of her fingers round one of the edges of the triangle. ' Touch it so,' she says. He promptly and delightedly imitates her. She then pulls all the figures out of their light-blue frames by means of a brass button in each, mixes them up on the table; and tells him to call her when he has them all in place again. The dark-blue cloth shows through the empty frame, so that it appears as if the figures had only sank down half an inch. While he continues to stare at this array, off goes the teacher.

" ' Is she not going to show him how to begin? '

" ' An axiom of our practical pedagogy is to aid the child only to be independent,' answers Dr. Montessori. ' He does not wish help.'

" Nor does he seem to be troubled. He stares a while at his array of blocks; yet his eye does not grow quite sure, for he carefully selects an oval from the mixed-up pile and tries to put it in the circle. It won't go. Then, quick as a flash, as if subconsciously rather than designedly, he runs his little forefinger around the rim of the figure and then round the edge of the empty space left in the light-blue frames of both the oval and the circle. He discovers his mistake at once, puts the figure into its place, and leans back a moment in his chair to enjoy his own cleverness before beginning with another. He finally gets them all into their proper frames, and instantly pulls them out again, to do it quicker and better next time.

" These blocks with the geometric insets are among the most valuable stimuli in the Casa dei Bambini. The vision and the touch become, by their use, accustomed to a great variety of shapes. It will be noted, too, that the child apprehends the forms synthetically, as given entities, and is not taught to recognize them by aid of even the simplest geometrical analysis. This is a point on which Dr. Montessori lays particular stress."

Now it is to be borne in mind that although, for the children, this is only a " game," as fascinating to them as the picture-puzzle is to their elders, their far-seeing teacher is utilizing it, far cry though it may seem, to begin to teach them to write. And here I realize that I have at last written a phrase for which my bewildered reader has probably been waiting in an astonished impatience. For of all the profound, searching, regenerating effects of the Montessori system, none seems to have made an impression on the public like the fact, almost a by-product of the method, that Montessori children learn to write and read more easily than others. I have heard Dr. Montessori exclaim in wonder many times over the popular insistence on that interesting and important, but by no means central, detail of her work; as though reading and writing were our only functions in life, as though we could get information and education only from the printed page, a prop which is already, in the opinion of many wise people, too largely used in our modern world as a substitute for first-hand, individual observation.

It cannot be denied, however, that the way Montessori children learn to write is very spectacular. The theory underlying it is far too complicated to describe in complete detail in a book of this sort, but for the benefit of the person who desires to run and read at the same time, I will set down a short-cut, unscientific explanation.

The inaccuracy and relative weakness of a little child's eyesight, compared to his sense of touch, has been already mentioned (page 57). This simple element in child physiology must be borne constantly in mind as one of the determining factors in the Montessori method of teaching writing. The child who is " playing " with the geometric insets soon learns, as we have seen from Miss Tozier's description, that he can find the shallow recess which is the right shape for the piece of wood which he holds in his hand if he will run the fingers of his other hand around the edge of his piece of wood and then around the different recesses.

It is hard for an ordinary adult really to conceive of the importance of this movement for a little child.

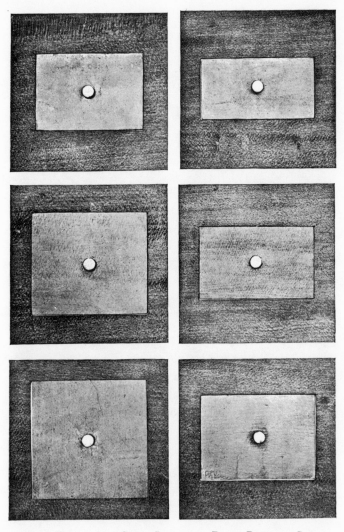

INSETS WHICH THE CHILD LEARNS TO PLACE BOTH BY SIGHT
AND BY TOUCH.

Indeed, so fixed is our usual preference for vision as a means of gaining information, that it gives one a very queer feeling to watch a child, with his eyes wide open, apparently looking intently at the board with its different-shaped recesses, but unable to find the one matching the inset he holds, until he has gone through that eerie, blind-man's motion with his finger-tips.

Now that motion, very frequently repeated, not only tells him where to fit in his inset, but, like all frequently repeated actions, wears a channel in his brain which tends, whenever he begins the action, to make him complete it in the way he always has done it. It can be seen that, if, instead of a triangle or a square, the child is given a letter of the alphabet and shown how to follow its outlines with his fingers in the direction in which they move when the letter is written, the brain channel and muscular habit resulting are of the utmost importance.

But before he can make any use of this, he needs to learn another muscular habit, quite distinct from (although always associated with) the mastery of the letters of the alphabet, namely, the mastery of the pencil. The exceeding awkwardness naturally felt by the child in holding this new implement for the first time, has nothing to do with his recognition of A or B, although it adds another great difficulty to his reproducing those letters. He must learn how to manage his pencil before he engages upon the much more complicated undertaking of constructing with it certain fixed symbols, just as he must learn how to walk before he can be sent on an errand. The old-fashioned way (still generally in use in Italy, and not wholly abandoned in all parts of our own country) was to force the child to fill innumerable copy-books with monotonous straight lines or " pot-hooks," a weariness of the spirit and a thorn in the flesh which any one who has suffered from it can describe feelingly. One way adopted by modern educators to avoid this dreary exercise is by frankly running away from the issue and postponing teaching children to write until a much more mature age than formerly, in the hope that general exercises in free-hand drawing will sufficiently supplement the general strengthening and steadying of the muscles which come with more mature development. It is an inaccurate but, perhaps, suggestive comparison to say that this is a little as though young children should not be taught how to walk because it is so hard for them to keep their balance, but made to wait until all their bones are mature.

Dr. Montessori has solved the difficulty by another use of the geometric insets. This time it is the hole left by the removal of one of the insets which is used. Suppose, for instance, that one chooses the triangular inset. It is set down on a piece of paper and the triangle is lifted out, leaving the paper showing through. The child is provided with colored crayons and shown how to trace around the outline

of the triangular-shaped piece of paper. The fact
that the metal frame stands up a little from the
paper prevents his at first wildly unsteady pencil
from going outside the triangle.   When he has
traced around the outline * with his blue crayon, he
lifts the frame up and there is the most beautiful
blue triangle, all the work of his own hands! He
usually gazes at this in delighted surprise, and then
it is suggested to him to fill in this outline with
strokes of his pencil.   He is allowed to make these
as he chooses, only being cautioned not to pass outside the line.   At first the crayon goes " every which
way," and the " drawings " are hardly recognizable
because the outline has been so overrun at every
point; but gradually the child's muscular control
is improved and finally carried to a very high degree
of perfection.   Regular, even parallel lines begin
to appear and the final result is as even as a Jap-
anese color-wash.   It is evident that in the course
of this work he makes of his own accord, with the
utmost interest animating each stroke, as many lines
as would fill hours and hours of enforced drudgery
over copy-books.   When, after much practice, the
muscles have learned almost automatically to control
fingers holding a pencil, that particular muscular
habit is sufficiently well-learned for the child to
begin on another enterprise.

Now of course, though it is most interesting to

* At first he traces only the outline of the inside figure. Later
the square frame is also outlined.

color triangles and circles, a child does not spend all his day at it.   Among other things which occupy and amuse him at this time is getting acquainted with the look and feel of the letters of the alphabet.   The children are presented, one at a time, sometimes only one a day, with large script letters, made of black sandpaper pasted on smooth white cards, and are taught how to draw their fingers over the letter in the direction taken when it is written.   At the same time the teacher repeats slowly and distinctly the sound of the letter, making sure that the child takes this in.

After this, the little Italian child, happy in the possession of a phonetically spelled language, has an easier time than our English-speaking children, who begin then and there their lifelong struggle with the insanities of English spelling.   But this is a struggle to which they must come under any system, and much less formidable under this than it has ever been before.   For the next step is, of course, to put these letters together into simple words.   There is no need to wait until a child has toiled all through the alphabet before beginning this much more interesting process.   As soon as he knows two letters he can spell Mamma.   There is no question as yet of his constructing the letters with his own hands.   He simply takes them from their separate compartments and lays them on the floor or table in the right order.   In handling them throughout all of these exercises the children are encouraged constantly to make that blind-man's motion of tracing around the letter.   The

rough sandpaper apparently shouts out information to the little finger-tips highly sensitized by the
tactile exercises, for the child nearly always corrects
himself more surely by touching than by looking at
his sandpaper alphabet.   Of course, the strongest of
muscular habits is being formed as he does this.

A pleasant variation on this routine is a test
of the child's new knowledge.   The teacher asks
him to give her B, give her D, P, M, etc.   The
letters are kept in little pasteboard compartments, a
compartment for all the B's, another for all the D's,
and so on.   The child, in answer to the teacher's request, looks over these compartments and picks out
from all the others the letter she has asked for.   This,
of course, seems only like a game to him, a variation
on hide-and-seek.

All these processes go on day after day, side by
side, all invisibly converging towards one end.   The
practice with the crayons, the recognition of the
letters by eye and touch, the revelation as to the
formation of words with the movable alphabet, are so
many roads leading to the painless acquisition of the
art of writing.   They draw nearer and nearer together, and then, one day, quite suddenly, the famous " Montessori explosion into writing " occurs.
The teacher of experience can tell when this explosion
is imminent.   First the parallel lines which the child
makes to fill and color the geometric figures become
singularly regular and even; second, his acquaintance
with the alphabet becomes so thorough that he recog-

nizes the letters by sense of touch only, and, third, he increases in facility for composing words with the movable alphabet. The burst into spontaneous writing usually comes only after these three conditions are present.

It usually happens that a child has a crayon in his hand and begins the motion of his fingers made as he traces around one of his sandpaper letters. But this time he has the pencil in his fingers, and the idea suddenly occurs to him, usually reducing him to breathless excitement, that if he traces on the paper with his pencil the form of the letters, he will be writing. In the twinkling of an eye it is done. He has written with his own hand one of the words which he has been constructing with the movable alphabet. He is usually as proud of this achievement as though he had invented the art of writing. The first children who were taught in this manner and who experienced this explosion into writing did really believe, I gather, that writing was something of their own invention. They rushed about excitedly to explain, to anyone who would listen, all about this wonderful new discovery: "Look! Look! You don't need the movable letters to make words. See, you just take a pencil or a piece of chalk, and draw the letters for yourself . . . as many as you please . . . anywhere!" And, in fact, for the first few days after this explosion, their teachers and mothers found writing "anywhere!" all over the house. The children were in a fever of excited pride. Since then, al-

though the first word always causes a spasm of joy,
children in a Children's Home are so used to seeing
the older ones writing and reading, that their own
feat is taken more calmly, as a matter of course.   It
really always takes place in this sudden way, however.   One day a child cannot write, and the next
he can.

The formation of the letters, so hard for children
taught in the old way, offers practically no difficulty
to the Montessori child.   He has traced their outline
so often with his finger-tips that his knowledge of
them is lodged where, in his infant organism, it belongs, in his muscular memory; so that when, pencil
in his well-trained hand, he starts his fingers upon an
action already so often repeated as to be automatic,
muscular habit and muscular memory do the rest.   He
does not need consciously to direct each muscle in
the action of writing, any more than a practised
piano-player thinks consciously of which finger goes
after which.   The vernacular phrase expressing this
sort of involuntary, muscular-memory facility is
literally true in his case, " He has done it so often
that he could do it with his eyes shut."   It is to be
noted that for a long time after this explosion into
writing, the children continue incessantly to go
through the three preparatory steps, tracing with
their fingers the sandpaper letters, filling in the
geometric forms and composing with the movable
alphabet.   These are for them what scales are for

the pianist, a necessary practice for "keeping the hand in." By means of constantly tracing the sandpaper letters the children write almost from the first the most astonishingly clear, firm, regular hand, much better than that of most adults of my acquaintance.

It is apparent, from even this short-hand account of this remarkably successful method, that children cannot learn to write by means of it without considerable (even if unconscious and painless) effort on their part, and without intelligence, good judgment, and considerable patience on the part of the teacher. The popular accounts of the miracles accomplished by Dr. Montessori's apparatus have apparently led some American readers to fancy that it is a sort of amulet one can tie about the child's neck, or plaster to apply externally, which will cause the desired effect without any further care. As a matter of fact, it is a carefully devised trellis which starts the child's sensory growth in a direction which will be profitable for the practical undertaking of learning how to write, a trellis invented and patented by Dr. Montessori, but which those of us who attempt to teach children must construct for ourselves on her pattern, following step by step the development of each of the children under our care.

And yet, although the Montessori apparatus does not teach children by magic how to write a good hand, in comparison with the methods now in use, it is really almost miraculous in its results. In our schools

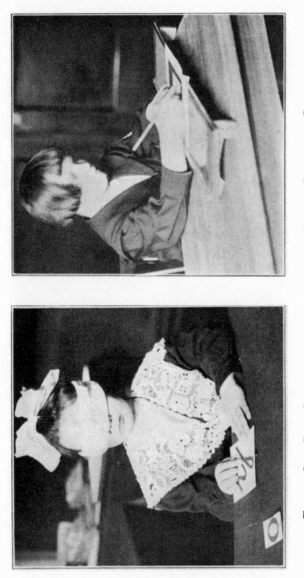

Tracing Geometrical Design.

Tracing Sand-Paper Letters.

children learn slowly to write (and how badly!) when they are seven or eight, cannot do it fluently until they are much older, and never do it very well, if the average handwriting of our high-school and college student is any test of our system. In the Montessori schools a child of four usually spends about a month and a half in the definite preparation for writing, and children of five usually only a month. Some very quick ones of this age learn to write with all the letters in twenty days. Three months' practice, after they once begin to write, is, as a rule, enough to steady their handwriting into an excellently clear and regular script, and, after six months of writing, a Montessori tot of five can write fluently, legibly, and (most important and revolutionary change) with pleasure, far beyond that usually felt by a child in, say, our third or fourth grades.

He has not only achieved this valuable accomplishment with enormous economy of time, but he has been spared, into the bargain, the endless hours of soul-killing drudgery from which the children in our schools now suffer. The Montessori child has, it is true, gone through a far more searching preparation for this achievement, but it has all been without any strain on his part, without any consciousness of effort except that which springs from the liveliest spontaneous desire. It has tired him, literally, no more than if he had spent the same amount of time playing tag.

I have heard some scientific talk which sounded to

my ignorant ears very profound and psychological, about whether this capacity of Montessori children to write can be considered as a truly " intellectual achievement," or only a sort of unconsciously learned trick. This is a fine theoretic distinction which I think most mothers will feel they can safely ignore. Whatever it is from a psychological standpoint, and however it may be rated in the Bradstreet of pure science, it is an inestimable treasure for our children.

Reading comes after writing in the Montessori system, and has not apparently as inherently close a connection with it as is sometimes thought. That is, a child who can form letters perfectly with his pencil and can compose words with the movable alphabet may still be unable to recognize a word which he himself has neither written nor composed. But, of course, with such a start as the Montessori system gives him, the gap between the two processes is soon bridged. There are various reasons why a detailed account of the Montessori method of teaching reading need not be given here. One is that this book is written for mothers and not teachers, and since the methods for teaching reading in our schools are much better than those used for teaching writing, mothers will naturally, as a rule, leave reading until the child is under a teacher. Furthermore, there is nothing so very revolutionary in the Montessori method in this regard and there exist already in this country several excellent methods for teaching reading. And yet a few notes on some features of the Montessori system will be of interest.

Like many variations of our own system it begins with the recognition of single words. At first these are composed with the movable alphabet. Later, when the child can interpret readily words composed in this way, they are written in large clear script on slips of paper. The child spells the word out letter by letter, and then pronounces these sounds more and more rapidly until he runs them together and perceives that he is pronouncing a word familiar to him. This is always a moment of great satisfaction to him and of encouragement to his teacher.

After this has continued until the children recognize single words quickly, the process is extended to phrases. Here the teacher goes very slowly, with great care, to avoid undue haste and lack of thoroughness. There is a danger here that the children will fall into the mechanical habit (familiar to us all) of reading aloud a page with great glibness, although the sense of the words has made no impression on their minds. To avoid this the Montessori Directress adopts the simple expedient of not allowing them at first to read aloud. She carries on, instead, a series of silent conversations with the children, writing on the board some simple request for an action on their part. " Please stand up," " Please shut your eyes," and so on. Later longer and more complicated sentences are written on slips of paper and distributed to the children. They read these to themselves (not being misled by their oral fluency into thinking they understand what they do not), and show that they have understood by performing the actions requested. In other words, these are short letters addressed by the teacher to the children, and answered by silent action on the part of the children. Like all of the Montessori devices, this is self-corrective. It is perfectly easy for the child to be sure whether he has understood the sentence or not, and his attention is fixed, not on pronouncing correctly (which has nothing to do with understanding the sentences before him), but on the comprehension of the written symbols. As for the teacher, she has an absolutely perfect check on the child. If he does not understand, he does not do the right thing. It means the elimination of the " fluent bluffer," a phenomenon not wholly unfamiliar to teachers, even when they are dealing with very young children.

CHAPTER VI

SOME GENERAL REMARKS ABOUT THE MONTESSORI APPARATUS IN THE AMERICAN HOME

THE first thing to do, if you can manage it, is to secure a set of the Montessori apparatus. It is the result of the ripest thought, ingenuity, and practical experience of a gifted specialist who has concentrated all her forces on the invention of the different devices of her apparatus. But there are various supplementary statements to be made which modify this simple advice.

One is, that the arrival in your home of the box containing the Montessori apparatus means just as much for the mental welfare of your children as the arrival in the kitchen of a box of miscellaneous groceries means for their physical health. The presence on the pantry shelf of a bag of the best flour ever made will not satisfy your children's hunger unless you add brains and good judgment to it, and make edible, digestible bread for them. There is nothing magical or miraculous about the Montessori apparatus. It is as yet the best raw material produced for satisfying the intellectual hunger of normal children from three to six, but it will have practically no effect on them if its use is not regulated by the most attentive care, supplemented by a keen and never-ceasing objective scrutiny of the children who are to use it. This is one reason why mothers find it harder to educate their children by the Montessori system (as by all other systems) than teachers do, for they have an age-long mental habit of clasping their little ones so close in their arms that, figuratively speaking, they never get a fair, square look at them.

This study of the children is an essential part of all education which Dr. Montessori is among the first pointedly and definitely to emphasize. The necessity for close observation of conditions before any attempt is made to modify them is an intellectual habit which is the direct result of the methods of positive sciences, in the study of which she received her intellectual training. Just as the astronomer looks fixedly at the stars, and the biologist at the protoplasm before he tries to generalize about their ways of life and action, so we must learn honestly and whole-heartedly to try to see what sort of children Mary and Bob and Billy *are*, as well as to love them with all our might. This should not be, as it is apt to be, a study limited to their moral characteristics, to seeing that Mary's fault is vanity and Bob's is indifference, but should be directed with the most passionate attention to their intellectual traits as well, to the way in which they naturally learn or don't learn, to the doors which are open, and those which are shut, to their intellectual interest. For

children of three and four have a life which it is no
exaggeration to call genuinely intellectual, and their
constant presence under the eyes of their parents
gives us a chance to know this, which helps to make
up for our lack of educational theory and experience
in which almost any teacher outstrips us.

There are no two plants, in all the infinity of
vegetable life, which are exactly alike.   There are
not, so geologists tell us, even two stones precisely
the same.   To lump children (even two or three children closely related) in a mass, with generalizations
about what will appeal to them, is a mental habit
that experience constantly and luridly proves to be
the extremest folly.   This does not mean individu-
alism run wild.   There are some general broad principles which hold true of all plants, and which we will
do well to learn from an experienced gardener.   All
plants prosper better out-of-doors than in a cellar,
and all children have activity for the law of their nature.   But lilies-of-the-valley shrivel up in the amount
of sunshine which supplies just the right conditions for nasturtiums, and your particular three-year-
old may need a much quieter (or more boisterous)
activity than his four-year-old sister.   Neither of
them may be, at first, in the least attracted by the
problem of the geometric insets, or by the idea of
matching colors.   They may not have reached that
stage, or they may have gone beyond it.   You will
need all your ingenuity and your good judgment to
find out where they are, intellectually, and what they

are intellectually.   The Montessori rule is never to
try to force or even to coax a child to use any part
of the apparatus.   The problem involved is explained
to him clearly, and if he feels no spontaneous desire
to solve it, no effort is made to induce him to undertake it.   Some other bit of apparatus is what, for the
moment, he needs, and one only wastes time in trying
to persuade him to feel an interest which he is, for
the time, incapable of.

If you doubt this, and most of us feel a lingering
suspicion that we know better than the child what he
wants, look back over your own school-life and confess to yourself how utterly has vanished from your
mind the information forced upon you in courses
which did not arouse your interest.   My own private
example of that is a course on "government."   I was
an ordinarily intelligent and conscientious child, and I
attended faithfully all the interminable dreary recitations of that subject, even filling a note-book with
selections from the teacher's remarks, and, at the
end of the course, passing a fairly creditable examination.   The only proof I have of all this is the rec-
ord of the examination and the presence, among my
relics of the past, of the note-book in my handwriting; for, among all the souvenirs of my school-
life, there is not one faintest trace of any knowledge
about the way in which people are governed.   I cannot even remember that I ever did know anything
about it.   My mind is a perfect, absolute blank on the
subject, although I can remember the look of the

schoolroom in which I sat to hear the lectures on it,
I can see the face of the teacher as plainly as though
she still stood before me, I can recall the pictures on
the wall, the very graining of the wood on my desk.
There is only no more recollection of the subject
than if the lectures had been delivered in Hin-
dustani. The long hours I spent in that classroom
are as wholly wasted and lost out of my all-too-short
life as though I had been thrust into a dark closet
for those three hours a week. Even the amount of
" discipline " I received, namely the capacity to sit
still and endure almost intolerable ennui, would have
been exactly as great in one case as in the other,
and would have cost the State far less.

All of us must have some such recollection of our
school-life to set beside the vivifying, exciting, never
to be forgotten hours when we first really grasped a
new abstract idea, or learned some bit of scientific
information thrillingly in touch with our own understandable lives; and we need no other proof of the
truth of the maxim, stated by all educators, but
stated and *constantly acted upon* by Dr. Montessori,
that the prerequisite of all education is the interest of
the student. There is no question here to be dis-
cussed as to whether he learns more or less quickly,
more or less well, according as he is interested or not.
The statement is made flatly by the Italian educator
that he does not, he cannot learn at all, anything, if
he is not interested. There is no use trying to call
in the old war-horse of " mental discipline " and say

that it is well to force him to learn whether he has an interest in the subject or not, because the fact is that he cannot learn without feeling interest; and the appearance of learning, the filled note-books, the attended recitations, the passed examinations, we all know in our hearts to be but the vainest of illusions and to represent only the most hopelessly wasted hours of our youth.

Dr. Montessori, with her usual bold, startlingly consistent acceptance as a practical guide to conduct of a fact which her reason tells her to be true, acts on this principle with her characteristic whole-souled fervor. If the children are not interested, it is the business of the educator to furnish something which will interest them (as well as instruct them) rather than to try to force their interest to center itself on some occupation which the educator has thought beforehand would turn the trick.* When we capture and try to tame a little wild creature of unknown habits (and is not this a description of each little new child?) our first effort is to find some food which will agree with him, and experimentation is always our first resort. We offer him all sorts of things

---

* A note here may perhaps clear up a possible misconception. It is to be remembered that all these statements about the necessity for interest in the child's mind refer only to *educative* processes. Occasions may arise when it is desirable that a child shall do something which does not interest him—for instance, sit still in a railway train until the end of the journey. But no one need think that he will ever acquire a taste for this occupation through being forced to it.

to eat, and observe which he selects.   It is true that we
do make some broad generalizations from the results
of our experiences with other animals, and we do not
try to feed a little creature who looks like a woodchuck on honey and water, nor a new variety of moth
on lettuce-leaves.   But even if the unknown animal
looks ever so close a cousin of the woodchuck family,
we do not try to force the lettuce-leaves down his
throat if, after a due examination of them, he shows
plainly that he does not care for them.   We cast
about to see what else may be the food he needs ; and
though we may feel very impatient with the need for
making all the troublesome experiments with diet, we
never feel really justified in blaming the little creature
for having preferences for turnip-tops, nor do we
have a half-acknowledged conviction that, perhaps, if
we had starved him to eat lettuce-leaves, it might have
been better for him.   We are only too thankful to
hit upon the right food before our little captive dies
of hunger.

Something of all this is supposed to go through the
mind of the Montessori mother as she refrains from
arguing with her little son about the advisability of
his being interested in one, rather than another, of
the Montessori contrivances ; and these considerations
are meant to explain to her the prompt acquiescence
of the Montessori teacher in the child's intellectual
" whims."   She is not foolishly indulging him to
make herself less trouble, or to please him.   She is
only trying to find out what his natural interest

is, so that she may pounce upon it and utilize it for teaching him without his knowing it.   She is only taking advantage of her knowledge of the fact that water runs down-hill and not up, and that you may keep it level by great efforts on your part, and even force it to climb, but that you can only expect it to work for you when you let it follow the course marked out for it by the laws of physics.   In other words, she sees that her business is to make use of every scrap of the children's interest, rather than to waste her time and theirs trying to force it into channels where it cannot run; to carry her waterwheel where the water falls over the cliff, and not to struggle to turn the river back towards the watershed.   And anyone who thinks that a Montessori teacher has "an easy time because she is almost never really teaching," underestimates grotesquely the amount of alert, keen ingenuity and capacity for making fine distinctions, required for this new feat of educational engineering.

On the other hand, the advanced modern educators who cry jealously that there is nothing new in all this, that it is the principle underlying their own systems of education, need only to ask themselves why their practice is so different from that of the Italian doctor, why a teacher who can force, coerce, coax, or persuade all the members of a class of thirty children to "acquire" practically the same amount of information about a given fixed number of topics within a given fixed period of time, is called a "good" teacher?   They will answer inevitably that chaos and anarchy in the educational world would result from any course of study less fixed than that in their schools.   And an impartial observer, both of our schools and of history, might reply that chaos and anarchy have been prophesied every time a more liberal form of government, giving more freedom to the individual, has been suggested, anywhere in the world.

In any case, the Montessori mother, with the newly acquired apparatus spread out before her, needs to gird herself up for an intellectual enterprise where she will need not only all the strength of her brain, but every atom of ingenuity and mental flexibility which she can bring to bear on her problem.   She will do well, of course, to fortify herself in the first place by a careful perusal of Dr. Montessori's own description of the apparatus and its use, or by reading any other good manual which she can find.   The booklet sent out with the apparatus gives some very useful detailed instructions which it is not necessary to repeat here, since it comes into the hands of everyone who secures the apparatus.   One of the main things for the Montessori mother to remember is that the teachers in the Casa dei Bambini are trained to make whatever explanations are necessary, as brief as possible, given in as few words as they can manage, and with good long periods of silence in between.

Much of the apparatus is so ingeniously devised that any normally inventive child needs but to have it set before him to divine its correct use. The buttoning-frames, and the solid and plane geometric insets need not a single word of explanation, even to start the child upon the exercise. But the various rods and blocks, used for the Long and Broad Stair and the Tower, are so much like ordinary building-blocks that, the first time they are presented, the child needs a clear presentation of how to handle them. This can be made an object-lesson conducted in perfect silence; although later, when the child begins to use the sandpaper numbers with them as he learns the series of numbers up to ten, he needs, of course, to be guided in this exercise.

With these rods and blocks especially, care should be taken to observe the Montessori rule that apparatus is to be used for its proper purpose only, in order to avoid confusion in the child's mind. He should never use the color spools, for instance, to build houses with. Not that, by any means, he should be coaxed to continue the exercises in color if he feels like building houses; but other material should be given him—a pack of cards, building-blocks, small stones, anything handy, but never apparatus intended for another exercise.

In the exercises for learning the difference between rough and smooth, the child needs at first a little guidance in learning how to draw his finger-tips *lightly* from left to right over the sandpaper strips; and in the exercises of discrimination between different fabrics, he needs someone to tie the bandage over

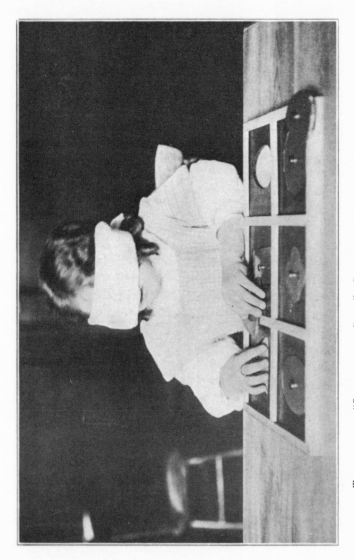

Training the "Stereognostic Sense"—Combining Motor and Tactual Images.

his eyes and, the first time, to show him how to set
to work.

A silent object-lesson, or a word or two, are needed
to show him how to separate and distinguish between
the pieces of wood of different weights in the baric
exercises, and a similar introduction is needed to the
cylindrical sound-boxes.

As he progresses both in age and ability, and begins some of the more complicated exercises, he needs
a little longer explanation when he begins a new exercise, and a little more supervision to make sure
that he has understood the problem.   In the later
part of the work with plane geometric insets, and in
the work with colored crayons, he needs occasional
supervision, not to correct the errors he makes, but
to see that he keeps the right aim in sight.   Of
course, when he begins work with the alphabet he
needs more real " teaching," since the names of the
letters must be told him, and care must be taken that
he learns firmly the habit of following their outlines
in the right direction, of having them right side up,
etc.   But throughout one should remember that most
" supervision " is meddling, and that one does the
child a real injury in correcting a mistake which, with
a little more time and experience, he would have been
able to correct for himself.   It is well to keep in
mind, also, that little children, some of them at least,
have a peculiarity shared by many of us adults, and
that is a nervousness under even silent inspection.   I
know a landscape painter of real ability who is re-

duced almost to nervous tears and certainly to para-
lyzed impotence, by the harmless presence of the
group of silent, staring spectators who are apt to
gather about a person making a sketch out of doors.
Even thoughwe may refrain from actually interfering
in the child's fumbling efforts to conquer his own lack
of muscular precision, we may wear on him nervously
if we give too close an attention to his efforts.   The
right thing is to show him (if necessary) what he is
to try to do, and then if it arouses his interest so
that he sets to work upon it, we will do well to busy
ourselves somewhat ostentatiously with something else
in the room.   Occasionally a child, even a little child,
has acquired already the habit of asking for help
rather than struggling with an obstacle himself.   The
best way to deal with this unfortunate tendency is to
provide simpler and simpler exercises until, through
making a very slight effort " all himself," the child
learns the joy of self-conquest and re-acquires his
natural taste for independence.   Most of us, with
healthy normal children, however, meet with no
trouble of this kind.   The average child of three, or
even younger, set before the solid geometric insets,
clears the board for action by the heartiest and most
instinctive rejection of any aid, suggestions, or even
sympathy.   His cry of "Let *me* do it!" as he
reaches for the little cylinders with one hand and
pushes away his would-be instructor with the other,
does one's heart good.

It is to be seen that Dr. Montessori's demand for

child-liberty does not mean unbridled and unregulated license for him, even intellectual license; nor does her command to her teachers to let him make his own forward advance mean that they are to do nothing for him. They may, indeed, frequently they must, set him carefully on a road not impossibly hard for him, and head him in the right direction. What they are not to do, is to go along with him, pointing out with a flood of words the features of the landscape, smoothing out all the obstacles, and carrying him up all the hills.

More important than any of the details in the use of the apparatus is the constant firm intellectual grasp on its ultimate purpose. The Montessori mother must assimilate, into the very marrow of her bones, the fundamental principle underlying every part of every exercise, the principle which she must never forget an instant in all the detailed complexity of its ingenious practical application. She is to remember constantly that the Montessori exercises are neither games to amuse the children (although they do this to perfection), nor ways for the children to acquire information (although this is also accomplished admirably, though not so directly as in the kindergarten work). They are, like all truly educative methods, means to teach the child how to learn. It is of no great importance that he shall remember perfectly the form of a square or a triangle, or even the sacred cube of Froebelian infant-schools. It is of the highest importance that he shall acquire the mental habit of observing quickly and accurately the form of any object he looks at or touches, because if he does, he will have, as an adult, a vision which will be that of a veritable superman, compared to the unreliable eyesight on which his parents have had to depend for information. It is of no especial importance that he shall learn quickly to distinguish with his eyes shut that a piece of maple the same size as a piece of pine is the heavier of the two. It is of the utmost importance that he shall learn to take in accurate information about the phenomena of the world, from whichever sense is most convenient, or from all of them at once, correcting and supplementing each other as they so seldom do with us badly trained adults.

CHAPTER VII

THE POSSIBILITY OF AMERICAN ADAPTATIONS OF, OR ADDITIONS TO, THE MONTESSORI APPARATUS

HOLDING firmly in mind the guiding principle formulated in the paragraph preceding, it may not be presumptuous for us, in addition to exercising our children with the apparatus devised by Dr. Montessori, to attempt to apply her main principles in ways which she has not happened to hit upon. She herself would be the first to urge us to do this, since she constantly reiterates that she has but begun the practical application of her theories, and she calls for the co-operation of the world in the task of working out complete applications suitable for different conditions.

It is my conviction that, as soon as her theories are widely known and fairly well assimilated, she will find, all over the world, a multitude of ingenious co-partners in her enterprise, people who, quite unconscious of her existence, have been for years approximating her system, although never doing so systematically and thoroughly. Is it not said that each new religion finds a congregation ready-made, of those who have been instinctively practising the as yet unformulated doctrines?

An incident in my own life which happened years ago, is an example of this. One of the children of the family, an adored, delicate little boy of five, fell ill while we were all in the country. We sent at once in the greatest haste to the city for a trained nurse, and while awaiting her arrival, devoted ourselves to the task of keeping the child amused and quiet in his little bed. The hours of heart-sickening difficulty and anxiety which followed can be imagined by anyone who has, without experience, embarked on that undertaking. We performed our wildest antics before that pale, listless little spectator, we offered up our choicest possessions for his restless little hands, we set in motion the most complicated of his mechanical toys; and we quite failed either to please or to quiet him.

The nurse arrived, cast one glance at the situation, and swept us out with a gesture. We crept away, exhausted, beaten, wondering by what possible miraculous *tour de force* she meant single-handed to accomplish what had baffled us all, and holding ourselves ready to secure for her anything she thought necessary, were it the horns of the new moon. In a few moments she thrust her head out of the door and asked pleasantly for a basket of clothes-pins, just common wooden clothes-pins.

When we were permitted to enter the room an hour or so later, our little patient scarcely glanced at us, so absorbed was he in the fascinatingly various angles at which clothes-pins may be thrust into each other's

clefts. When he felt tired, he shut his eyes and
rested quietly, and when returning strength brought
with it a wave of interest in his own cleverness, he
returned to the queer agglomeration of knobby wood
which grew magically under his hands.   Now Dr. Montessori could not possibly have used that " sensory
exercise," as they have no clothes-pins in Italy,
fastening their washed garments to wires, with knotted
strings ; and the nurse was probably married with
children of her own before Dr. Montessori opened
the first Casa dei Bambini ; but that was a true Montessori device, and she was a real " natural-born "
Montessori teacher.   And I am sure that everyone
must have in his circle of acquaintances several persons who have such an intuitive understanding of
children that Dr. Montessori's arguments and theories will seem to them perfectly natural and axiomatic.
One of my neighbors, the wife of a farmer, a plain
Yankee woman who would be not altogether pleased
to hear that she is bringing up her children according
to the theories of an inhabitant of Italy, has, by the
instinctive action of her own wits, hit upon several
inventions which might, without surprising the Directress, be transferred bodily to any Casa dei Bambini.   All of her children have gone through what she
calls the " folding-up fever," and she has laid away in
the garret, waiting for the newest baby to grow up to
it, the apparatus which has so enchanted and instructed all the older ones.   This " apparatus," to
use the unfortunately mouth-filling and inflated name

which has become attached to Dr. Montessori's simple expedients, is a set of cloths of all shapes and sizes, ranging from a small washcloth to an old bedspread.

When the first of my neighbor's children was a little over three, his mother found him, one hot Tuesday, busily employed in "folding up," that is, crumpling and crushing the fresh shirtwaists which she had just laboriously ironed smooth. She snatched them away from him, as any one of us would have done, but she was nimble-witted enough to view the situation from an impersonal point of view which few of us would have adopted. She really "observed" the child, to use the Montessori phrase; she put out of her mind with a conscious effort her natural, extreme irritation at having the work of hours destroyed in minutes, and she turned her quick mind to an analysis of the child's action, as acute and sound as any the Roman psychologist has ever made. Not that she was in the least conscious of going through this elaborate mental process. Her own simple narration of what followed, runs: " I snatched 'em away from him and I was as mad as a hornit for a minit or two. And then I got to thinkin' about it. I says to myself, ' He's so little that 'tain't nothin' to him whether shirtwaists are smooth or wrinkled, so he couldn't have taken no satisfaction in bein' mischievous. Seems 's though he was wantin' to fold up things, without really sensin' what he was doin' it *with*. He's seen me fold things up. There's other things than shirtwaists he could fold, that 'twouldn't

do no harm for him to fuss with.' And I set
th' iron down and took a dish-towel out'n the
basket and says to him, where he set cryin', ' Here,
Buddy, here's somethin' you can fold up.' And he
set there for an hour by the clock, foldin' and un-
foldin' that thing."

That historic dish-towel is still among the " apparatus " in her garret. Five children have learned
deftness and exactitude of muscular action by means
if it, and the sixth is getting to the age when his
mother's experienced eye detects in him signs of the
" fever."

Now, of course, the real difference between that
woman and Dr. Montessori, and the real reason why
Dr. Montessori's work comes in the nature of a revelation of new forces, although hundreds of " natural
mothers " long have been using devices strongly re-
sembling hers, is that my neighbor hasn't the slightest
idea of what she is doing and she has a very erroneous
idea of why she is doing it, inasmuch as she regards
the fervor of her children for that fascinating sense
exercise, as merely a Providential means to enable
her to do her housework untroubled by them. She
could not possibly convince any other mother of any
good reason for following her examples because she is
quite ignorant of the good reason.

Dr. Montessori, on the other hand, with the keen
self-consciousness of its own processes which characterizes the trained mind, is perfectly aware not
not only of what she is doing, but of a broadly

fundamental and wholly convincing philosophical reason for doing it; namely, that the child's body is a machine which he will have to use all his life in whatever he does, and the sooner he learns the accurate and masterful handling of every cog of this machine the better for him.

Now, whenever frontier conditions exist, people generally are forced to learn to employ their senses and muscles much more competently than is possible under the usual modern conditions of specialized labor performed almost entirely away from the home; and though for most of us the old-fashioned conditions of farm-life so ideal for children, the free roaming of field and wood, the care and responsibility for animals, the knowledge of plant-life, the intimate acquaintance with the beauties of the seasons, the enforced self-dependence in crises, are impossibly out of reach, we can give our children some of the benefits to be had from them by analyzing them and seeing exactly which are the elements in them so tonic and invigorating to child-life, and by adapting them to our own changed conditions. There are even a few items which we might take over bodily. A number of families in my acquaintance have inherited from their ancestors odd " games " for children, which follow perfectly the Montessori ideas. One of them is called the " hearth-side seed-game " and is played as the family sits about the hearth in the evening,—though it might just as well be played about a table in the dining-room with the light turned low. Each child is given a cup of mixed grains, corn, wheat, oats, and buckwheat. The game is a competition to see who can the soonest, by the sense of touch only, separate them into separate piles, and it has an endless fascination for every child who tries it—if he is of the right age, for it is far too fatiguing for the very little ones. Another family makes a competitive game of the daily task of peeling the potatoes and apples needed for the family meals. Once the general principle of the " Montessori method " is grasped, there is no reason why we should not apply it to every activity of our children. Indeed Dr. Montessori is as impatient as any other philosopher, of a slavishly close and unelastic interpretation of her ideas. Furthermore, it is to be remembered that the set of Montessori apparatus was not intended by its inventor to represent all the possible practical applications of her theories. For instance, there are in it none of the devices for gymnastic exercises of the whole body which she recommends so highly, but which as yet she has been able to introduce but little into her schools. Here, too, what she would wish us to do is to make an effort to comprehend intelligently what her general ideas are and then to use our own invention to adapt them to our own conditions.

A good example of this is the enlightenment which comes to most of us, after reading her statement about the relative weakness of little children's legs. She calls our attention to the fact that the legs of the newborn baby are the most negligible members he possesses, small and weak out of all proportion to his body and arms. Then with an imposing scientific array of carefully gathered statistics, she proves that this disproportion of strength and of size continues during early childhood, up to six or seven. In other words, that a little child's legs are weaker and tire more quickly than the rest of him, and hence he craves not only those exercises which he takes in running about in his usual active play, but others which he can take without bearing all his weight on his still rather boneless lower extremities.

This fact, although doubtless it has been common property among doctors for many years, was entirely new to me; and probably will be to many of the mothers who read this book, but an ingenious person has only to hear it to think at once of a number of exercises based on it. Dr. Montessori herself suggests a little fence on which the children can walk along sideways, supporting part of their weight with their arms. She also describes a swing with a seat so long that the child's legs stretched out in front of him are entirely supported by it, and which is hung before a wall or board against which the child presses his feet as he swings up to it, thus keeping himself in motion. These devices are both so simple that almost any child might have the benefit of them, but even without them it is possible to profit by the above bit of physiological information, if it is only by restraining ourselves from forbidding a child the instinctive gesture we must all have seen, when he throws himself on his stomach across a chair and kicks his hanging legs. If all the chairs in the house are too good to allow this exercise, or if it shocks too much the adult ideas of propriety, a bench or kitchen-chair out under the trees will serve the same purpose.

Everyone who is familiar with the habits of natural children, or who remembers his own childish passions, knows how they are almost irresistibly fascinated by a ladder, and always greatly prefer it to a stair-case. The reason is apparent. After early infancy they are not allowed to go upstairs on their hands and knees, but are taught, and rightly taught, to lift the whole weight of their bodies with their legs, the inherent weakness of which we have just learned. Of course this very exercise in moderation is just what weak legs need; but why not furnish also a length of ladder out of doors, short enough so that a fall on the pile of hay or straw at the foot will not be serious? As a matter of fact, you will be astonished to see that even with a child as young as three, the hay or straw is only needed to calm your own mind. The child has no more need of it than you, nor so much, his little hands and feet clinging prehensilely to the rounds of the ladder as he delightedly ascends and descends this substitute for the original tree-home.

The single board about six inches wide and three or four inches from the ground (a length of joist or studding serves very well) along which the child walks and runs, is an exercise for equilibrium which is elsewhere described (page 149). This can be

varied, as he grows in strength and poise, by having
him try some of the simpler rope-walking tricks of
balance, walking on the board with one foot, or backward, or with his eyes shut. It is fairly safe to say,
however, that having provided the board, you need
exercise your own ingenuity no further in the matter. The variety and number of exercises of the sort
which a group of active children can devise goes far
beyond anything the adult brain could conceive.
The exercises with water are described (page
151). These also can be varied to infinity, by the
use of receptacles of different shapes, bottles with
wide or narrow mouths, etc.

The folding-up exercises seem to me excellent, and
the hearth-side seed-game is, in a modified form, already in use in the Casa dei Bambini. Small, low
see-saws, the right size for very young children, are
of great help in aiding the little one to learn the
trick of balancing himself under all conditions; and
let us remember that the sooner he learns this all-
important secret of equilibrium, the better for him,
since he will not have the heavy handicap of the bad
habit of uncertain, awkward, misdirected movements,
and he will never know the disheartening mental distress of lack of confidence in his own ability deftly,
strongly, and automatically to manage his own body
under all ordinary circumstances.

A very tiny spring-board, ending over a heap of
hay, is another expedient for teaching three- and
four-year-olds that they need not necessarily fall in

a heap if their balance is quickly altered. If this simple device is too hard to secure, a substitute which any woman and even an older child can arrange for a little one, is a long thin board, with plenty of " give " to it, supported at each end by big stones, or by two or three bits of wood. The little child bouncing up and down on this and " jumping himself off " into soft sand, or into a pile of hay, learns unconsciously so many of the secrets of bodily poise that walking straight soon becomes a foregone conclusion.

One of the blindfold games in use in Montessori schools is played with wooden solids of different shapes, cubes, cylinders, pyramids, etc. The blindfolded child picks these, one at a time, out of the pile before him and identifies each by his sense of touch. In our family this has become an after-dinner game, played in the leisure moments before we all push away from the table and go about our own affairs, and managed with a napkin for blindfold, and with the table-furnishings for apparatus.

The identification of different stuffs, velvet, cotton, satin, woolen, etc., can be managed in any house which possesses a rag-bag. I do not see why the possession of a doll, preferably a rag-doll, should not be as valuable as the Montessori frames. Most dolls are so small that the hooks and eyes and the buttons and buttonholes on their minute garments are too difficult for little fingers to manage, whereas a doll which could wear the child's own clothes would cer-

tainly teach him more about the geography of his
raiment than any amount of precept. I can lay no
claim to originality in this idea. It was suggested
to my mind by the constant appearance in new costumes of the big Teddy-bear of a three-year-old
child, whose impassioned struggles with the buttons of
her bear's clothes forms the most admirable of self-
imposed manual gymnastics.

Lastly, it must not be forgotten that the " sets of
Montessori apparatus " must be supplemented by several articles of child-furniture. There is not in it
the little light table, the small low chair so necessary
for children's comfort and for their acquiring correct, agreeable habits of bodily posture. Such little
chairs are easily to be secured but, alas! rarely found
in even the most prosperous households. We must not
forget the need for a low washstand with light and
easily handled equipment; the hooks set low enough
for little arms to reach up to them, so that later we
shall not have to struggle with the habit fixed in the
eight-year-old boy, of careless irresponsibility about
those of his clothes which are not on his back; the
small brooms and dust-pans so that tiny girls will
take it as a matter of course that they are as much
interested as their mothers in the cleanliness of a
room; in short, all the devices possible to contrive to
make a little child really at *home* in his father's house.

CHAPTER VIII

SOME REMARKS ON THE PHILOSOPHY OF
THE SYSTEM

WHEN I first began to understand to some extent the thoroughgoing radicalism of the philosophy of liberty which underlies all the intricate detail of Dr. Montessori's system, I used to wonder why it went home to me with such a sudden inward conviction of its truth, and why it moved me so strangely, almost as the conversion to a new religion. This Italian woman is not the first, by any means, to speak eloquently of the righteousness of personal liberty. As far back as Rabelais' "Fay ce que vouldras " someone was feeling and expressing that. Even the righteousness of such liberty for the child is no invention of hers. Jean Jacques Rousseau's " Émile," in spite of all its disingenuous evading of the principle in practice, was founded on it in theory ; and Froebel had as clear a vision as any seer, as Montessori herself, of just the liberty his followers admit in theory and find it so hard to allow in practice.

Why, then, should those who come to Rome to study the Montessori work, stammerers though they might be, wish, all of them, to go away and prophesy? For almost without exception this was the common result among the widely diverse national types I saw in Rome; always granting, of course, that they had seen one of the good schools and not those which present a farcical caricature of the method.

In thinking the matter over since, I have come to the conclusion that the vividness of inward conviction arises from the fact that the founder of this " new " philosophy bases it on the theory of democracy; and there is no denying that the world to-day is democratic, that we honestly in our heart of hearts believe, as we believe in the law of gravity, that, on the whole, democracy, for all its shortcomings, has in it the germ of the ideal society of the future.

Now, our own democracy was based, a hundred or so years ago, on the idea that men reach their highest development only when they have, for the growth of their individuality, the utmost possible freedom which can be granted them without interfering with the rights and freedom of others. Little by little during the last half-century the idea has grown that, inasmuch as women form half the race, the betterment of the whole social group might be hastened if this beneficial principle were applied to them.

If you will imagine yourself living sixty or so years ago, when, to conservative minds, this idea of personal liberty for women was like the sight of dynamite under the foundations of society, and to radical minds shone like the dawn of a brighter day, you can imagine how startling and thrilling is the first glimpse of its application to children. I felt, during the beginning of my consideration of the question, all the sharp pangs of intellectual growing-pains which must have racked my grandfather when it first occurred to him that my grandmother was a human being like himself, who would very likely thrive under the same conditions which were good for him. For, just as my grandfather, in spite of the sincerest affection for his wife, had never conceived that he might be doing her an injury by insisting on doing her thinking for her, so I, for all my love for my children, had never once thought that, by my competent, loving " management " of them, I might be starving and stunting some of their most valuable moral and intellectual qualities.

In theory I instantly granted this principle of as much personal liberty as possible for children. I could not help granting it, pushed irresistibly forward as I was by the generations of my voting, self-governing ancestors ; but the resultant splintering upheaval of all my preconceived ideas about children was portentous.

The first thing that Dr. Montessori's penetrating and daring eye had seen in her survey of the problem of education, and the fact to which she devotes throughout her most forceful, direct, and pungent explanation, had simply never occurred to me, in spite of Froebel's mild divination of it; namely, that children are nothing more or less than human beings. I was as astonished by this fact as I was amazed that I had not thought of it myself; and I instantly perceived a long train of consequences leading off from it to a wholly unexplored country. True, children are not exactly like adults; but then, neither are women exactly like men, nor are slow, phlegmatic men exactly like the red-headed, quick-tempered type; but they all belong to the genus of human beings, and those principles which slow centuries of progress have proved true about the genus as a whole hold true about subdivisions of it. Children are much weaker physically than most adults, their judgment is not so seasoned by experience, and their attention is more fitful. Hence, on the whole, they need more guidance than grown-ups. But, on the other hand, the motives, the instincts, the needs, the potential capacities of children are all human and nothing but human. Their resemblances to adults are a thousand times more numerous and vital than their differences. What is good for the one must, in a not excessively modified form, be good for the other.

With this obvious fact firmly in mind, Dr. Montessori simply looked back over history and drew upon the stores of the world's painfully acquired wisdom as to the best way to extract the greatest possibilities from the world's inhabitants. If it is true, she reasoned, that men and women have reached their highest development only when they have had the utmost possible liberty for the growth of their individualities, if it is true that slavery has been the most ruinously unsatisfactory of all social expedients, both for masters and slaves, if society has found it necessary for

its own good to abolish not only slavery but caste
laws and even guild rules; if, with all its faults, we
are agreed that democracy works better than the
wisest of paternal despotisms, then it ought to be
true that in the schoolroom's miniature copy of society there should be less paternal despotism, more
democracy, less uniformity of regulation and more,—
very much more,—individuality.

Therefore, although we cannot allow children as
much practical freedom as that suitable for men of
ripe experience, it is apparent that it is our first duty
as parents to make every effort to give them as full
a measure of liberty as possible, exercising our utmost
ingenuity to make the family life an enlightened
democracy. But this is not an easy matter. A
democracy, being a much more complicated machine
than an autocracy, is always harder to organize and
conduct. Moreover the family is so old a human institution that, like everything else very old, it has
acquired barnacle-like accretions of irrelevant tradition. Elements of Russian tyranny have existed in
the institution of the family so long that our very
familiarity with them prevents us from recognizing
them without an effort, and prevents our conceiving
family life without them; quite as though in this age
of dentistry, we should find it difficult to conceive of
old age without the good old characteristic of tooth-
lessness. To renovate this valuable institution of the
family (and one of the unconscious aims of the Montessori system is nothing more or less than the renova-

tion of family life), we must engage upon a daily
battle with our own moral and intellectual inertia,
rising each morning with a fresh resolve to scrutinize
with new eyes our relations to our children. We must
realize that the idea of the innate " divine right of
parents " is as exploded an idea as the " divine right
of kings." Fathers and mothers and kings nowadays
hold their positions rightfully only on the same conditions as those governing other modern office-holders,
that they are better fitted for the job than anyone
else.

I speak from poignant personal experience of the
difficulty of holding this conception in mind. When
I said above that I " saw at once a long train of
consequences following this new principle of personal
liberty for children," I much overstated my own acu-
men; for I am continually perceiving that I saw
these consequences but very vaguely through the
dimmed glasses of my unconscious, hidebound con-
servatism, and I am constantly being startled by the
possibility of some new, although very simple application of it in my daily contact with the child-
world. A wholesome mental exercise in this connection is to run over in one's mind the dramatic changes
in human ideas about family life which have taken
place gradually from the Roman rule that the father
was the governor, executioner, lawgiver, and absolute
autocrat, down to our own days. For all our clinging to the idea of a closely intimate family-life, most
of us would turn with horror from any attempt to re-

turn to such tyranny as that even of our own Puritan
forebears. It is possible that our descendants may
look back on our present organization with as much
astonished and uncomprehending revulsion.

The principle, then, of the Montessori school is
the ideal principle of democracy, namely, that human
beings reach their highest development (and hence
are of most use to society) only when for the growth
of their individuality they have the utmost possible
liberty which can be granted them without interfering
with the rights of others. Now, when Dr. Montessori,
five years ago, founded the first Casa dei Bambini, she
not only believed in that principle but she saw that
children are as human as any of us; and, acting with
that precipitate Latin faith in logic as a guide to
practical conduct which is so startling to Anglo-
Saxons, she put these two convictions into actual
practice. The result has electrified the world.

She took as her motto the old, old, ever-misunder-
stood one of " Liberty! "—that liberty which we still
distrust so profoundly in spite of the innumerable
hard knocks with which the centuries have taught us it
is the only law of life. She was convinced that the
" necessity for school discipline " is only another expression of humanity's enduring suspicion of that
freedom which is so essential to its welfare, and that
schoolroom rules for silence, for immobility, for uniformity of studies and of results, are of the same
nature and as outworn as caste rules in the world
of adults, or laws against the free choice of residence

for a workman, against the free choice of a profession
for women, against the free advance of any individual
to any position of responsibility which he is capable
of filling.

All over again in this new field of education Dr.
Montessori fought the old fight against the old idea
that liberty means red caps and riots and guillotines.
All afresh, as though the world had never learned the
lesson, she was obliged to show that liberty means
the only lasting road to order and discipline and self-
control. Once again, for the thousandth time, people
needed to be reminded that the reign of the tyrant
who imposes laws on human souls from the outside
(even though that tyrant intends nothing but the best
for his subjects and be called " teacher "), produces
smothered rebellion, or apathy, or broken submissive-
ness, but never energetic, forward progress.

For this constant turning to that trust in the
safety of freedom which is perhaps the only lasting
spiritual conquest of our time, is the keynote of her
system. This is the real answer to the question,
" What is there in the Montessori method which is
so different from all other educational methods? "
This is the vital principle often overlooked in the
fertility of invention and scientific ingenuity with
which she has applied it.

This reverence for the child's personality, this supreme faith that liberty of action is not only safe
to give children, but is the prerequisite of their
growth, is the rock on which the edifice of her sys-

tem is being raised. It is also the rock on which the barks of many investigators are wrecked. When they realize that she really puts her theory into execution, they cry out aghast, " What! a school without a rule for silence, for immobility, a school without fixed seats, without stationary desks, where children may sit on the floor if they like, or walk about as they please; a school where children may play all day if they choose, may select their own occupations, where the teacher is always silent and in the background—why, that is no school at all—it is anarchy! "

One seems to hear faint echoes from another generation crying out, " What! a society without hereditary aristocracy, without a caste system, where a rail-splitter may become supreme governor, where people may decide for themselves what to believe without respect for authority, and may choose how they wish to earn their livings, . . . this is no society at all! It is anarchy! "

Dr. Montessori has two answers to make to such doubters. One is that the rule in her schools, like the rule in civilized society, is that no act is allowed which transgresses against the common welfare, or is in itself uncomely or offensive. That the children are free, does not mean that they may throw books at each other's heads, or light a bonfire on the floor, any more than free citizens of a republic may obstruct traffic, or run a drain into the water-supply of a town. It means simply that they are subject to no *unnecessary* restraint, and above all to no meddling with their instinctive private preferences. The second answer, even more convincing to hard-headed people than the first, is the work done in the Case dei Bambini, where every detail of the Montessori theory has been more than proved, with an abundance of confirmatory detail which astonishes even Dr. Montessori herself. The bugbear of discipline simply does not exist for these schools. By taking advantage of their natural instincts and tendencies, the children are made to perform feats of self-abnegation, self-control, and collective discipline, impossible to obtain under the most rigid application of the old rules, and, as for the amount of information acquired unconsciously and painlessly by those babies, it is one of the fairy-stories of modern times.

CHAPTER IX

APPLICATION OF THIS PHILOSOPHY TO AMERICAN HOME LIFE

NATURALLY, the question which concerns us is, how the spiritual discoveries made in this new institution in a far-away city of Italy, can be used to benefit our own children, in our own everyday, American family life. It must be stated uncompromisingly, to begin with, that they can be applied to our daily lives only if we experience a " change of heart." The use of the vernacular of religion in this connection is not inappropriate, for what we are facing, in these new principles, is a new phase of the religion of humanity. We are simply, at last, to include children in humanity, and since despotism, even the most enlightened varieties of it, has been proved harmful to humanity, we are to abstain from being their despots, even their paternal, wise, and devoted despots. This does not mean that they are not to live under some form of government of which we are the head. We have as much right to safeguard their interests against their own weaknesses as society has to safeguard ours, in forbidding grade railways in big cities for instance, but we have no more right than society has to interfere with inoffensive individual tastes, preferences, needs, and, above all, initiative.

At this point I can hear in my mind's ear a chorus of indignant parents' voices, crying out that nothing is further from their theory or practice than despotism over the children, and that, so far from ruling their little ones, they are the absolute slaves of their offspring (forgetting that in many cases there is no more despotic master than a slave of old standing). To answer this natural protest I wish here to be allowed a digression for the purpose of attempting a brief analysis of a trait of human egotism, the understanding of which bears closely on this phase of the relations of parent and child. I refer to the instinctive pleasure taken by us all in the dependence of someone upon us.

This is so closely connected with benevolence that it is usually wholly unrecognized as a separate and quite different characteristic. Even when it is seen, it is identified only by those who suffer from it, and any intimation of its existence on their part savors so nearly of ingratitude that they have not, as a rule, ventured to complain of what is frequently an almost intolerable tyranny. Just as it is the spiteful member of a family who is the only one to blurt out home-truths which run counter to the traditional family illusions, so it is only a thoroughly bad-tempered analyst, one who takes a malicious pleasure in dwelling on human meannesses, who can perform the useful function of diagnosing this little suspected, very prevalent, human vice.

Here is the sardonic Hazlitt, derisively relieving his mind on the subject of benefactors. ". . . Benefits are often conferred out of ostentation or pride. As the principle of action is a love of power, the complacency in the object of friendly regard ceases with the opportunity or the necessity for the manifest display of power; and when the unfortunate protégé is just coming to land and expects a last helping hand, he is, to his surprise, pushed back in order that he may be saved from drowning once more. You are not haled ashore as you had supposed by those kind friends, as a mutual triumph, after all your struggles and their exertions on your behalf. It is a piece of presumption in you to be seen walking on terra firma; you are required at the risk of their friendship to be always swimming in troubled waters that they may have the credit of throwing out ropes and sending out life-boats to you without ever bringing you ashore. The instant you can go alone, or can stand on your own ground, you are discarded."

Now the majority of us in these piping times of mediocrity have no grounds, fancied or real, for assuming the rôle of tyrannical Providence to other people. But the instinct, in spite of the decreased opportunity for its exercise, is none the less alive in our hearts; and when chance throws in our way a little child, our primitive, instinctive affection for

whom confuses in our minds the motives underlying
our pseudo-benevolent actions, do we not wreak upon
it unconsciously all that latent desire to be depended
upon, to be the stronger, to be looked up to, to
gloat over the weakness of another?

If this seems an exaggerated statement, consider
for a moment the real significance of the feeling
expressed by the mothers we have all met, when they
cry, " Oh, I can't *bear* to have the babies grow up!"
and when they refuse to correct the pretty, lisping,
inarticulate baby talk.   I have been one of those
mothers myself, and I certainly would have regarded
as malicious and spiteful any person who had told
me that my feelings sprang from almost unadul-
terated egotism, and that I " couldn't bear to have
the babies grow up " because I wanted to continue
longer in my complacent, self-assumed rôle of God,
that I wished to be surrounded by little sycophants
who, knowing no standard but my personality, could
not judge me as anything but infallible, and that I
was wilfully keeping the children granted me by a
kind Heaven as weak and dependent on me as possible that they might continue to secrete more food
for my egotism.

What I now see to be a plain statement of the
ugly truth underlying my sentimental reluctance
to have the babies grow up would have seemed to
me the most heartless attack on mother-love.   It
now occurs to me that mother-love should be something infinitely more searching and subtle.   Modern

society with its enforced drains and vaccinations and milk inspection and pure-food laws does much of the physical protecting which used to fall to the lot of mothers. Our part should not be, like bewildered bees, to live idly on the accumulation of virtues achieved for us by the hard won battles of our ancestors against their lower physical instincts; but to catch up the standard and advance into the harder battle against the hidden, treacherous ambushes of egotism, to conceive a new, high devotion for our children, a devotion which has in it courage for them as well as care for them; which is made up of faith in their better, stronger natures, as well as love for them, and which begins by the ruthless slaughter, so far as we can reach it, of the selfishness which makes us take pleasure in their dependence on us, rather than in seeing them grow (even though it may mean away from us) in the ability wisely to regulate their own lives. We must take care that we mothers do not treat our children as we reproach men for having treated women, with patronizing, enfeebling protection. We must learn to wish, above all things, to see the babies grow up since there is no condition (for any creature not a baby) more revolting than babyishness, just as there is no state more humiliating (for any but a child) than childishness. Let us learn to be ashamed of our too imperious care, which deprives them of every chance for action, for self-reliance, for fighting down their own weaknesses, which snatches away from them every opportunity to strengthen themselves by overcoming obstacles. We must learn to see in a little child not only a much-loved little body, informed by a will more or less pliable to our own, but a valiant spirit, longing for the exercise of its own powers, powers which are different from ours, from those of every human being who has ever existed.

There is no danger that in combating this subtle vice, we will fall back into the grosser one of physical tyranny over women, children, or the poor. That step forward has been taken conclusively. That question has been settled for all time and has been crystallized in popular opinion. We may still tyrannize coarsely over the weak, but we are quite conscious that we are doing something to be ashamed of. We can therefore, without fear of reactionary setbacks, devote ourselves to creating a popular consciousness of the sin of moral and intellectual tyranny.

Now all this reasoning has been conducted by means of abstract ideas and big words. It may seem hardly applicable to the relations of an affectionate parent with his three-year-old child. How, practically, concretely, at once, to-day, can we begin to avoid paternal despotism over little children?

To begin with, by giving them the practical training necessary to physical independence of life. Anyone who knows a woman who lived in the South during the old régime must have heard stories of the pathetic, grotesque helplessness to which the rich white popula-

tion was reduced by the presence and personal service
of the slaves . . . the grown women who could not
button their own shoes, the grown men who had never
in their lives assembled all the articles necessary for
a complete toilet. Dr. Montessori says, " The para-
lytic who cannot take off his boots because of a pathological fact, and the prince who dare not take them
off because of a social fact, are in reality reduced to
the same condition." How many mothers whose
willing fingers linger lovingly over the buttons and
strings and hooks and eyes of the little costume are
putting themselves in the pernicious attitude of the
slave? How many other bustling, competent, quick-
stepping mothers, dressing and undressing, washing
and feeding and regulating their children, as though
they were little automata, because " it's so much
easier to do it for them than to bother to teach them
how to do it," are reducing the little ones to a state
of practical paralysis? As if ease were the aim of
a mother in her relations to her child! It would be
easier, as far as that is concerned, to eat the child's
meals for it; and a study of the " competent " brand
of mother almost leads one to suspect that only the
physical impossibility of this substituted activity
keeps it from being put into practice. The too
loving mother, the one who is too competent, the
one who is too wedded to the regularity of her household routine, the impatient mother, the one who is
" no teacher and never can tell anybody how to do
things," all these diverse personalities, though actu-

ated by quite differing motives, are doing the same thing, unconsciously, benevolently, overbearingly insisting upon living the child's life for him.

But it is evident that simply keeping our hands off is not enough. To begin with the process of dressing himself, the first in order of the day's routine, a child of three, with no training, turned loose with the usual outfit of clothes, could never dress himself in the longest day of the year. And here, with a serious problem to be solved, we are back beside the buttoning boy of the Children's Home. The child must *learn how* to be independent, as he must learn how to be anything else that is worth being, and the only excuse for existence of a parent is the possibility of his furnishing the means for the child to acquire this information with all speed. Let us take a long look at the buttoning boy over there in Rome and return to our own three-year-old for a more systematic survey of his problem, which is none other than the beginning of his emancipation from the prison of babyishness. Let him learn the different ways of fastening garments together on the Montessori frames if you have them, or in any other way your ingenuity can devise. Old garments of your own, put on a cheap dress form, are not a bad substitute for that part of the Montessori apparatus, or the large doll suggested on page 115 may serve.

Then apply your mind, difficult as that process is for all of us, to the simplification of the child's costumes, even if you are led into such an unheard-

of innovation as fastening the little waists and dresses
up the front. Let me wonder, parenthetically, why
children's clothes should all be fastened at the back?
Men manage to protect themselves from the weather
on the opposite principle.

Then, finally, give him time to learn and to practise
the new process; and time is one of the necessary
elements of life most often denied to little children,
who always take vastly longer than we do to complete
a given process. I am myself a devoted adherent of
the clock, and cannot endure the formless irregularity
of a daily life without fixed hours, so that I do not
speak without a keen realization of the fact that
time cannot be granted to little children to live their
own lives, without our undergoing considerable in-
convenience, no matter how ingeniously we arrange
the matter. We must feel a whole-hearted willingness to forego a superfluity in life for the sake
of safeguarding an essential of life. When I feel
the temptation, into which my impatient temperament is constantly leading me, to perform some
action for a child which he would better do for himself, because his slowness interferes with my household schedule, I bring rigorously to mind the Montessori teacher who did not tuck in the child's napkin.
And I severely scrutinize the household process, the
regularity of which is being upset, to see if that
regularity is really worth a check to the child's
growth in self-dependence.

Once in a while it really does seem to me, on

mature consideration, that regularity is worth that
sacrifice, but so seldom as to be astonishing. One
of the few instances is the regularity of the three
meals a day. This seems to be an excellent means
of inculcating real social feeling in the child, of
making him understand the necessity for occasional
sacrifices of individual desires to benefit the common
weal. One should take care not to neglect or pass
over the few genuine opportunities in the life of a
little child, when he may feel that in common with
the rest of the family he is making a sacrifice which
counts for the sake of the common good.

But most other situations yield very different
results when analyzed. For instance, if a child must
dress in a cold room it is better for an adult to
stuff the little arms and legs into the clothes with
all haste, rather than run the risk of chilling the
child. But as a rule, if the conditions are really
honestly examined, these two alternatives are seen
not to be the only ones. He is set perhaps to dress
in a cold room because we have a tradition that it
is " messy " and " common " to have dressing and
undressing going on anywhere except in a bedroom.
The question I must then ask myself is no longer,
" Is there not danger that the child will take cold
if I give him time to dress himself? " but, " Is the
ordered respectability of my warm parlor worth a
check to my child's normal growth? "

And it is to some such quite unexpected question
that one is constantly led by the attempt really to

analyze the various restrictions we put upon the
child's freedom to live his own life. These restrictions multiply in such a perverse ratio with the
material prosperity and conventionality of our lives
that it is a truism that the children of the very poor
fare better than ours in the opportunities offered
them for the development of self-reliance, self-control, and independence, almost the most valuable outfit for the battle of life a human being can have.

It is impossible, of course, to consider here all
the processes of the child's day in as minute detail
as this question of his morning toilet. But the same
procedure of " hands off " should be followed, because
*help that is not positively necessary is a hindrance to
a growing organism.* It is well to put strings for your
vines to climb up, but it does them no good to have you
try to " help " them by pulling on the tips of the
tendrils. The little child should be allowed time to
wash his own face and hands, to brush his teeth, and
to feed himself, although it would be quicker to
continue our Strasbourg goose tradition of stuffing
him ourselves. He should, as soon as possible, learn
to put on and take off his own wraps, hat, and
rubbers. He should carry his own playthings, should
learn to open and shut doors, go up and down stairs
freely, hang up his own clothes (hooks placed low
must not be forgotten), and look himself for articles
he has misplaced.

Adults who, for the first time, try this régime
with little children are astonished to find that it is

not the patience of the little child, but their own, which is inadequate. A child (if he is young enough not to have acquired the invalid's habit of being waited upon) will persevere unendingly through a series of grotesquely awkward attempts, for instance, to climb upon an adult's chair. The sight of this laborious attempt to accomplish a perfectly easy feat reduces his quick-stepping, competent mother to nervous fidgets, requiring all her self-control to resist. She is almost irresistibly driven to rushing forward and lifting him up. If she does, she is very apt to see him slide to the floor and begin all over again. It is not elevation to the chair which he desires. It is the capacity to attain it himself, unaided, which is his goal, a goal like all others in his life which his mother cannot reach for him.

And if all this sounds too troublesome and complicated, let it be remembered that the Children's Home looms close at hand, ominously ready to devote itself to making conditions exactly right for the child's growth, never impatient, with no other aim in life and no other occupation but to do what is best for the child. If we are to be allowed to keep our children with us, we must prove worthy the sacred trust.

For, practically, the highly successful existence of the Casa dei Bambini, keeping the children as it does all day, takes for granted that the average parent cannot or will not make the average home into a place really suited for the development of

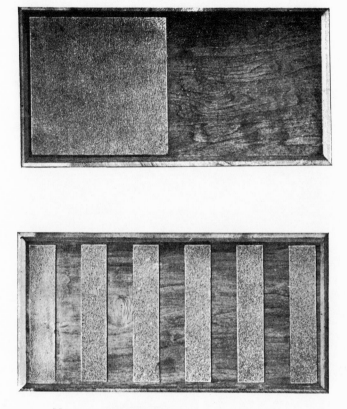

MATERIALS FOR TEACHING ROUGH AND SMOOTH.

small children. It is visibly apparent that, as far
as physical surroundings are concerned, he is Gulli-
ver struggling with the conditions of Brobdingnag.
He eats his meals from a table as high for him as
the mantelpiece would be for us, he climbs up and
down stairs with the painful effort we expend on the
ascent of the Pyramids, he gets into an armchair as
we would climb into a tree, and he can no more alter
the position of it than we could that of the tree.

As for the conduct of life, he is considered
" naughty " if he interferes with adult occupations,
which, going on all about him all the time and being
entirely incomprehensible to him, are very difficult to
avoid; and he is " good " like the " good Indian "
according to the degree of his silent passivity. When
we return after a brief absence and inquire of a little
child, " Have you been a good child? " do we not
mean simply, " Have you been as little inconvenient
as possible to your elders? " To most of us who
are honest with ourselves it comes as rather a surprise that this standard of virtue should not be the
natural and inevitable one.

I leave to the last chapter the question, a most
searching and painful one for me, as to whether the
Casa dei Bambini will not ultimately be the Home
for all our children, and here confine myself to the
statement, which no unprejudiced mind can deny, that
such an institution, arranged as it has been with
the most single-hearted desire to further the children's interests, is now better adapted for child-life

than our average homes, into which children may be welcomed lovingly, but which are adapted in every detail of their material, intellectual, and spiritual life for adults only. It is my firm conviction that, in my own case, a working compromise may be effected, thanks to my alarmed jealousy of the greater perfection of the Montessori Children's Home; but I realize that it required the alarming sight and study of that institution to make me see that I was forcing my children to live under a great many unnecessary restrictions. And, if there is one thing above all others to be kept in mind by a convert to these new ideas it is that an *unnecessary restriction in a child's life is a crime*. The most puritanical soul among us must see that there are quite enough necessary restrictions for the child, if they are all recognized and rigorously obeyed, to serve as disciplinary forces to the most turbulent nature.

CHAPTER X

SOME CONSIDERATIONS ON THE NATURE OF "DISCIPLINE"

WITH the last affirmation of the preceding chapter I have brought myself to another bed-rock principle of this new religion of childhood, one which at first I was unable to understand and hence to accept. In my very blood there runs that conviction of the necessity for discipline which colored so profoundly all early New England life. At the sight of this too-pleasant and too-smiling world of children, some old Puritan of an ancestor sprang to life in me and cried out sourly, " But it's good for children to do what they don't like to do, and to keep on with something after they want to stop. They must in later life. They should begin now."

The answer to this objection is one I have had practically to work out for myself, since the Italian exponents of the system, having back of them an unbroken line of life-loving and life-trusting Latin forefathers, found it practically impossible to understand what was in my mind. There was much talk of "discipline" in their discussion of the theories of the method; but evidently they did not attach the same meaning to the word as the one I had been trained to use. This fact led me to meditate on what I myself really meant by discipline: a process of definition which, as it always does, clarified my ideas and proved them in some respects quite different from what I had thought them.

Discipline means, of course, "the capacity for self-control." I had no sooner formulated this definition than I saw that I had been, in my practical use of the word, omitting half of it, and that the vital half. It was not discipline I had been vainly seeking at the Casa dei Bambini, it was compulsion.

Now, compulsion is a force very much handier to use in education than self-control, since it depends on the adult and not on the child, and practically any adult with a club (physical or moral) can compass it, if the child in his power is small enough. But the most elementary experience of life proves that the effects of compulsion last exactly as long as the physical or moral club can be applied. Evidently its use can scarcely prepare the child for the searching tests of independent adult life when no one has any longer even a pseudo-right to club him into moral action.

And yet self-control, like all other vital processes of individual life, is tantalizingly elusive and subtle. My untrained mind, face to face at last with the real problem, despaired of securing this real self-control and not the valueless compulsory obedience to external force or persuasion with which I had been confusing it. I saw that it is secured in the Children's

Home and betook myself once more to an examination of their methods.

Their method for solving this problem is like the one they use in all other problems of child-life. They use the adult brain to analyze minutely all the complex processes involved, and then they begin at the beginning to teach the children all the different actions, one after another.

For instance, the capacity for close, consecutive attention to any undertaking is a very valuable form of self-control and self-discipline (one which a good many adults have never mastered). The natural tendency of childhood, as of all untrained humanity, is for flightiness, for mental vagrancy, for picking up and fitfully dropping an enterprise. It is obvious that the sternest of external so-called discipline cannot lay a finger on this particular mental fault, because all it can command is physical obedience, which ceases when the compulsion is no longer active. In the Children's Home, the child is provided with a task so exactly suited to the instinctive needs of his growing organism, that his own spontaneous interest in it overcomes his own equally spontaneous aversion to mental concentration. Later on in life he must learn to concentrate mentally, whether he feels a strong spontaneous interest in the subject or not; but it is evident that he cannot do that, if he has not learned first to control his wandering wits when the subject does interest him. And that this last is not the perfectly easy undertaking it seems, is apparent when one considers all the hopelessly flighty women there are in the world, who could not, to save their lives, mentally concentrate on anything. The Montessori apparatus sets a valuable vital force in the child's own intellectual make-up to master an undesirable instinct, and naturally the valuable force grows stronger with every exercise of its power, just as a muscle does. The little boy who was so much interested in his buttoning-frame that he stuck to his enterprise from beginning to end without so much as glancing up at the activities of the other children, showed real self-control, even though it was not associated with the element of pain which my grim ancestors led me to think was essential.

It is true that self-control in the face of pain or indifference is a necessary element in adult moral and intellectual life, but it now appears that, like every other factor in life, it must start from small beginnings and grow slowly. The buttoning boy showed not only self-control, but the only variety of it which a baby is capable of manifesting. When I had the notion that I ought (for his own good, of course) to demand of him self-control in the face of pain, even of a very small pain, I was asking something which he could not as yet give, and of which compulsory obedience could only obtain an empty and misleading appearance, an appearance really harmful to the child's best interests since it completely blinded me to the fact that he had not made the least beginning towards attaining a real self-control. He must

begin slowly to learn self-control, as he must begin
slowly to learn how to walk. I am quite satisfied if
he takes a single step at first, because I know that is
the essential. If he can do that, he will ultimately
learn to climb a mountain. If he can overcome the
naturally vagrant impulses of his mind through intellectual interest (for it is none other) in the completion of his task of buttoning up the cloth on his
frame, he has begun a mental habit the value of
which cannot be overestimated, and which will later,
in its full development, make it possible for him to
master calculus without the agonizing, too-tardy effort at mental self-control which embittered my own
struggle with that subject.

From time immemorial, the child himself has always instinctively used in his games and plays this
method of learning self-control and mental concentration, as much as adults would allow him. The admirable, thoroughgoing concentration of a child on a
game of marbles or ball is proverbial; but while the
rest of us, with some unsystematic exceptions, have
looked idly on at this great natural stream of mental
vigor pouring itself out in profusion before our eyes,
Dr. Montessori has stepped in with an ingeniously
devised waterwheel and set it to work.

The child in the Casa dei Bambini advances from
one scientifically graded stage of mental self-control
to the next, from the buttoning-frames to the geometric insets, from these to their use in drawing and
the control of the pencil, and then on into the mas-

tery of the alphabet, always with a greater and greater control of the processes of his mind.

The control of the processes of his body are learned in the same analyzed, gradual progression from the easy to the difficult. He learns in the "lesson of silence" how to do nothing with his body, an accomplishment which his fidgety elders have never acquired; he learns in all the sensory exercises the complete control of his five servants, his senses; and in moving freely about the furniture suited to his size, in handling things small enough for him to manage, in transferring objects from one place to another, he learns how to go deftly through all the ordinary operations of everyday life.

This physical adroitness has a vitally close relation to discipline of all sorts. When we say to the average, untrained, muscularly uncontrolled child of four, "Now do sit still for a while!" we are making a request about as reasonable as though we cried, "Do stand on your head!" And then we shake him or reprove him for not obeying what is for him an impossible command. By so doing we start in his mind the habit, both of not obeying and of being punished for it; and as Nature is exuberant in her protective devices, he very soon grows a fine mental callous over his capacity for remorse at not obeying. The effort required to accede to our request is entirely too great for him, even if he wholly understands what we wish, which is often doubtful. And because he often has been forced to disobey a command to do something

impossible, he falls into the way of disobeying a
command which is within his powers.   The Montessori training makes every impassioned attempt to
teach a child exactly how to do a thing before he
is requested to do it.

We give a child the enormously compendious command, " Don't be so careless! " without reflecting
that it is about as useful and specific an exhortation
as if one should cry to us, " Do be more virtuous! "
Dr. Montessori is continually admonishing us to use
our grown-up brains to analyze into its component
parts the child's carelessness, so that, part by part, it
can be corrected.   Suppose that it has manifested
itself (as it not infrequently does) by a reckless
plunge across the room, carrying a plateful of cookies
which have most of them fallen to the floor by the end
of the trip.   Almost without exception, what we all
cry impatiently to a child, even to a very little child,
under those circumstances, is " For mercy's sake, *do*
look at what you're doing!" which is, considered at
all analytically, exactly what it is our business as his
leaders and guides in the world to do for him.

A little reflection on the subject makes us realize, in
spite of the sharpness of our reproof to him, that he
takes no pleasure in spilling the cookies and falling
over the chairs; that is, that he had no set purpose to
do this, instead of walking correctly across the room
and setting the plate down on the table.   The question
we should ask ourselves, is obviously, " Why then, did
he do all those troublesome and careless things?"   Ob-

viously because we were requiring him to go through a complicated process, the separate parts of which he has not mastered; as though a musician should command us to play the chromatic scale of D minor, and then blame us for the resultant discord. He should have taught us a multitude of things before requiring such a complicated achievement,—how to hold our fingers over the piano-keys, how to read music, how to play simpler scales.

The child with the cookie-plate needs, in the first place, a course of exercises in learning to walk in a straight line directly to the spot where he means to go, exercises continued until this process becomes automatic, so that the greatest haste on his part will not send him reeling about as most children (and a considerable number of their ill-trained elders) do when they undertake to move from one side of the room to another.

How can he learn to do this? Dr. Montessori suggests drawing a chalk-line on the floor and having the children play the " game " (either with or without music) of trying to walk along it without stepping off. I myself, remembering the forbidden joys of my reckless childhood in walking the top-rail of a fence, have tried the expedient of providing a less dangerous top-rail laid flat on the ground. Did any healthy child ever need more than one chance to walk along railway tracks? The objection in the past to these exercises has been that they were connected with something dangerous and undesirable. I do not blame my parents for forbidding me to try to balance myself either on the top-rail of a fence or on a rail-way track. Both of these were highly risky diver-sions. But it does seem odd that neither they nor I ever thought of providing, in some safe form, the exercises in equilibrium so violently craved by all healthy children. A narrow board, or length of so-called "two-by-four" studding, laid on the ground, furnishes a diversion as endlessly entertaining for a child of three as the most dangerously high fence-rail for an older child, and the never-failing zest with which a little child practises balancing himself on this narrow "sidewalk" is a proof that the exercise is one for which he unconsciously felt a need.

Another trick of equilibrium, which is hard for a little child, is to lift one foot from the floor and perform any action without falling over. If he is provided with a loose rope-end, hanging where he can easily reach it, his parent and guardian can sug-gest any number of entertaining things to do while his equilibrium is assured by his grasp on the rope. My experience has been that one suggestion is enough. The child's invention does the rest. Another exer-cise which is of great benefit for very little children is to walk backwards, a process which needs no more gymnastic apparatus than a helping hand from father or mother, an apparatus which is equally effect-ive in teaching a young child the fascinating game of crossing one foot over the other without falling down.

Does all this physical training of tiny children

seem too remote from the older child who spilled the cookies? He stands at the end of the road over which the balancing, backward-walking, highly entertained three-year-old is advancing.

Although it is not mentioned in any Montessori suggestions I have seen (possibly because of the difficulty of managing it in a schoolroom), it occurred to me one day that water is a neglected but very valuable factor in training a little child to accuracy of muscular movement. This reflection occurred to me just after I had instinctively led away a little child from a basin of water in which I had " caught her " dabbling her hands. Making a desperate effort to put into practice my new resolution to question myself sharply each time that I denied a child any activity he seemed to desire, I perceived that in this case, as so often, I was acting traditionally, without considering the essential character of the situation. I could not, of course, allow the child to dabble in that basin of water, there, because she would be apt to spatter it on the floor and to get her clothes wet. But on that warm summer day, why could I not set her outdoors on the grass, with a bit of oilcloth girded about her waist so that she should not spoil her dress? Her evident interest in the water was an indication of a natural force which it might be possible to utilize to give her some muscular training which would entertain her at the same time. When I really came to think about it, there is nothing inherently wicked in playing in water.

For the almost superhuman effort necessary to use reason about a fact the outlines of which are dulled by familiarity, I was rewarded many times over by the discovery of a " sensory exercise " which apparently is of the highest value. The child in question, provided with a pan of water, and various cups and jelly-molds of different sizes, which I snatched at random from the kitchen-shelf, was in a state of silent bliss. She filled the little cups up to the brim, she lifted them with an anxious care which no exhortation of mine could have induced her to apply, she drank from them, she poured their contents into each other, discovering for herself that the smaller ones must be emptied into the bigger ones and not vice versa, she filled them again with a spoon. At first she did all this very clumsily, although always with the most painstaking care, but as the days went on with repetitions of this game, her dexterity became astonishing, as was her eternal interest in the monotonous proceeding.

Now she is not only kept quiet and happy for about an hour a day by this amusement, and she has not only learned to fill and handle her little cups and jelly-molds very deftly, but the operation of drinking out of a water-glass at the table is of a simplicity fairly beneath her contempt. I smile to see our guests gasp and dodge in dismay as, with the reckless abandon of her age, she grasps her water-glass with one hand, not deigning even to look at it, and conveys it to her lips. But as a matter of fact, no matter how hastily or carelessly she does this, she almost never spills a drop. The control of utensils containing liquids has been so thoroughly learned by her muscles in the long hours of happy play with her little cups that it is perfectly automatic. She no more spills water from her glass than I fall down on the floor when I cross a room, even though I may be quite absent-minded about that undertaking.

CHAPTER XI

MORE ABOUT DISCIPLINE, WITH SPECIAL REGARD TO OBEDIENCE

I MUST stop at this point and devote a paragraph or two to laying the ghost of another Puritan ancestor who demands, " But where does the discipline come in here, if it is all automatic and unconscious? Why sneak exactitude of muscular action into the child's life by the back door, so to speak? Would it not be better for her moral nature to command her outright not to spill the water from her glass at table, and force her to use her will-power by punishing her if she does? "

There are several answers to this searching question, which is by no means so simple and direct as it sounds. The most obvious one is the retort brutal, i.e., that a great many generations have experimented with that simple method of training children, with the result that family life has been considerably embittered and the children very poorly trained. In other words, that practical experience has shown it to be a very bad method indeed and in use only because we know no better one.

One of the reasons why it is bad is because it confuses two radically different activities in the child's life, including both under one far too-sweeping com-

mand.   The child's ability to handle a glass of
water is an entirely different function from its willingness to obey orders.   To require of its nascent
capacities at the same instant a new muscular skill
and the moral effort necessary to obey a command is
to invite almost certain failure.   Worse than this, and
in fact as bad as anything can be, the result of this
impossibly compendious command is to bring about a
hopeless confusion in the child's mind which means
unnecessary nervous tension and friction and the
beginning of an utterly deplorable mental habit of
nervous tension and irritated resistance in the child's
mind, whenever a command is given.   That this instinct of irritated resistance is not a natural one is
proved by the happily obedient older children in the
Casa dei Bambini in Rome.   Furthermore, anyone
who will, under ordinary circumstances, try the simple experiment of asking a little child (too young to
have acquired this bad mental habit) to perform some
operation which he has thoroughly mastered, will be
convinced that obedience in itself involves no pain to a
child.

As to the second demand of my Puritan ancestor,
which runs, " And force her to use her will-power by
punishment," the same flat denial must be given that
proposition.   Experience proves that you can prevent
a child from performing some single special action
by means of external punishment, but that stimulat-
ing the proper use of the will-power is something
entirely different.   Apparently the will-power is more

apt to be perverted into grotesque and unprofitable shapes by the use of punishment than to be encouraged into upright, useful, and vigorous growth.

And here it is well to question our own hearts deeply to make sure that we really wish, honestly, without mental reservations, to stimulate the will-power of our children—their will-power, be it remembered, not our own. Is there, in the motives which actuate our attempts at securing obedience from children, a trace of the animal-trainer's instinct? For, though it is true that children are little animals, and that they can be successfully trained by the method of the animal-trainer, it is not to be forgotten that they are trained by those methods only to feats of exactly the same moral and intellectual caliber as those performed by trick dogs and cats. They are forced to struggle blindly, and wholly without aid, towards whatever human achievements they may later accomplish, with the added disadvantage of the mental habit either of sullen dissembled revolt or crushed mental servility, according to their temperaments.

The end and aim of the horse-breaker's effort is to create an animal who will obey literally, with no volition of his own, any command of any human being. The conscientious parent who faces squarely this ultimate logical conclusion of the animal-trainer's system, must see that his own aim, being entirely opposed to that, must be attained by very different means; and that, since his final goal is to produce a being wholly and wisely self-governing, the sooner the child can be induced to begin the exercise of the faculty of self-government, the more seasoned in experience it will be when vital things begin to depend on it.

It is highly probable that in the heart of the modern parent of the best type, if there is still some of the animal-trainer's instinct, he is quite and honestly unconscious of it and would be ashamed of it if he recognized it. I think most of us can say sincerely that we have no conscious wish for anything but the child's best welfare. But in saying this, we admit at once that our problem is vastly more subtle and complicated than the horse-breaker's, and that we are in need of every ray of light from any source possible.

The particular, vivifying truth which we must imprint on our minds in this connection is that spontaneity of action is the absolute prerequisite for any moral or intellectual advance on the part of any human being. Nor is this, though so constantly insisted upon by Dr. Montessori, any new invention of hers. Dimly felt, it has regulated more or less the best action of the best preachers, the best teachers and lawgivers since the beginning of the world. Pestalozzi formulated it in the hard saying, all the more poignant because it came from a man who had devoted himself with such passionate affection to his pupils, " I have found that no man in God's wide earth is able to help any other man. Help must come from the bosom alone." Froebel, in all his general remarks on education, states this principle clearly. Finally, it has been crystallized in the homely adage of old wives, " Every child's got to do its own growing."

We all admit the truth of this theory. What is so startling about Dr. Montessori's attitude towards it, is that she really acts upon it! More than that, she expects us to act on it, all the time, in all the multiform crises of our lives as parents, in this intricate problem of discipline and the training of the will-power as well as in the simpler form of physically refraining from interfering with the child's efforts to feed and dress himself.

And yet it is natural enough that we should find at first sight such general philosophic statements rather vague and remote, and not at all sufficiently reassuring as we stand face to face with the problem of securing obedience from a lively child of three. We may have seen how we overlooked the obvious reason why a child who *cannot* obey a command will not; and we may be quite convinced that the first step in securing both self-control and obedience from a child is to put the necessary means in his power ; and yet we may be still frankly at a loss and deeply apprehensive about what seems the hopeless undertaking of directly securing obedience even after the child has learned how to obey. All that Dr. Montessori has done for us so far is to call our attention to the fact, which we did not in the least perceive before, that a child is no more born into the world with

a full-fledged capacity to obey orders, than to do a
sum in arithmetic. But though we agree that we must
first teach him his numbers before expecting him to
add and subtract, how, we ask ourselves anxiously,
can we be in the least sure that he will be willing to
use his numbers to do sums with, that he will be willing to utilize his careful preparatory training when
it comes to the point of really obeying orders.

At this juncture I can recommend from successful
personal experience a courageous abandonment of
our traditional attitude of deep distrust towards life,
of our medieval conviction that desirable traits can
only be hewed painfully out across the grain of
human nature. The old monstrous idea which underlay all schooling was that the act of educating himself was fundamentally abhorrent to a child and that
he could be forced to do it only by external violence.
This was an idea, held by more generations of school-
teachers and parents than is at all pleasant to consider, when one reflects that it would have been swept
out upon the dump-heap of discarded superstitions
by one single, unprejudiced survey of one normal
child under normal conditions.

Dr. Montessori, carrying to its full extent a theory
which has been slowly gaining ground in the minds of
all modern enlightened teachers, has been the first to
have the courage to act without reservation on the
strength of her observation that the child prefers
learning to any other occupation, since the child is
the true representative of our race which does ad-

vance, even with such painful slowness, away from ignorance towards knowledge. Now, in addition she tells us just as forcibly, that they prefer right, orderly, disciplined behavior to the unregulated disobedience which we slanderously insist is their natural taste. As a result of her scientific and unbiased observation of child-life she informs us that our usual lack of success in handling the problems of obedience comes because, while we do not expect a child at two or three or even four to have mastered completely even the elements of any other of his activities, we do expect him to have mastered all the complex muscular, nervous, mental, and moral elements involved in the act of obedience to a command from outside his own individuality.

She points out that obedience is evidently a deep-rooted instinct in human nature, since society is founded on obedience. Indeed, on the whole, history seems to show that the average human being has altogether too much native instinct to obey anyone who will shout out a command; and that the advance from one bad form of government to another only slightly better, is so slow because the mass of grown men are too much given to obeying almost any positive order issued to them. Going back to our surprised recognition of the child as an inheritor of human nature in its entirety, we must admit that obedience is almost certainly an instinct latent in children.

The obvious theoretic deduction from this reasoning is, that we need neither persuade nor force a child to obey, but only clear-sightedly remove the various moral and physical obstructions which lie in the way of his obedience, with the confident expectation that his latent instinct will develop spontaneously in the new and favorable conditions.

When we plant a bean in the ground we do not feel that we need to try to force it to grow; indeed, we know very well that we can do nothing whatever about that since it is governed entirely by the presence or absence in the seed of the mysterious element of life; nor do we feel any apprehension about the capacity of that smooth, small seed, ultimately to develop into a vine which will climb up the pole we have set for it, will blossom, and bear fruit. We know that, barring accidents (which it is our business as gardeners to prevent), it cannot do anything else, because that is the nature of beans, and we know all about the nature of beans from a long acquaintnce with them.

We would laugh at an ignorant, city-bred person gardening for the first time, who, the instant the two broad cotyledons showed above the ground, began tying strings to them to induce them to climb his pole. Our advice to him would be the obvious counsel, " Leave them alone until they grow their tendrils. You not only can't do any good by trying to induce those first primitive leaves to climb, but you may hurt your plant so that it will never develop normally."

The question seems to be, whether we will have the

courage and good sense to take similar sound advice
from a more experienced and a wiser child-gardener.
Dr. Montessori not only expounds to us theoretically
this doctrine that the child, properly trained, will
spontaneously obey reasonable orders suited to his
age with a prompt willingness which grows with his
growth, but she shows us in the garden of her schools,
bean-poles wreathed triumphantly with vines to the
very top.   Or, to drop a perhaps too-elaborated
metaphor, she shows us children of three or four who
willingly obey suggestions suited to their capacities,
developing rapidly and surely into children of six and
seven whose obedience in all things is a natural and
delightful function of their lives.   She not only says
to us, " This theory will work in actual practice,"
but, " It *has* worked.   Look at the result! "

Of course the crux of the matter lies in that phrase,
" proper training."   It means years of patient, intelligent, faithful effort on the part of the guardian,
to clear away from before the child the different obstacles to the free natural growth of this, as of all
other desirable instincts of human nature.   To give
our children this " proper training " it is not enough
to have intellectually grasped the theory of the Montessori method.   With each individual child we have
a fresh problem of its application to him.   Our
mother-wits must be sharpened and in constant use.
Dr. Montessori has only compiled a book of recipes,
which will not feed our families, unless we exert ourselves, and unless we provide the necessary ingredients

of patience, intelligence, good judgment, and devotion.

The prize which seems possible to attain by such efforts makes them, however, worthy of all the time and thought we may possibly put upon them. Apparently, judging by the results obtained in the Casa dei Bambini among Italian children, and by Miss George in her school for American children, there is no more need for the occasional storms of temper or outbreaks of exasperated egotism which are so familiar to all of us who care for children, than there is for the occasional " fits of indigestion," " feverishness," or " teething-sickness " the almost universal absence of which in the lives of our scientifically-reared children so astonishes the older generation.

For the notable success of Miss George's Tarrytown school disposes once and for all of the theory that " it may work for Italians, but not with our naturally self-indulgent, spoiled American children." Fresh from the Casa dei Bambini in Rome, I visited Miss George's Children's Home and, except for the language, would have thought myself again on the Via Giusti. The same happy, unforced interest in the work, the same Montessori atmosphere of spontaneous life, the same utter unconsciousness of visitors, the same astonishing industry.

When theoretically by talk and discussion with experts on the subject and practically by the sight of the astonishing results shown in the enlightenment and self-mastery of the older children who had been

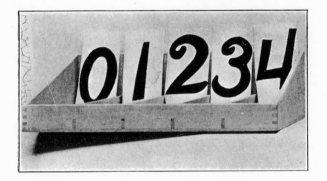

Counting Boxes.

trained in the system, I was led towards the conviction that children really have not that irresistible tendency towards naughtiness which my Puritan blood led me unconsciously to assume, but that their natural tendency is on the whole to prefer to do what is best for them, I felt as though someone had tried to prove to me that the world before my eyes was emancipating itself from the action of some supposedly inexorable natural law.

Naturally, being an Anglo-Saxon, an inhabitant of a cold climate, and the descendant of those troublesome Puritan forefathers, who have interfered so much with the composition of this book, I could not, all in a breath, in this dizzying manner lose that firm conviction of Original Sin which, though no longer insisted upon openly in the teachings of the church, which I no longer attend as assiduously as my parents, still is, I discovered, a very vital element in my conception of life.

No, the doctrine of Original Sin is in the very marrow of my New England bones, but, as a lover of my kind, I rejoice to be convinced of the smallness of its proportion in relation to other elements of human nature, and I bear witness gladly that I never saw or heard of a single case of wilful naughtiness among all the children in the Casa dei Bambini in Rome.   And though I still cling unreasonably to my superstition that there is, at least in some American children, an irreducible minimum of the quality which our country people picturesquely call " The Old

Harry," I am convinced that there is far, far less of it than I supposed, and I am overcome with retrospective remorse for all the children I have misjudged in the course of my life.

To put it statistically, I would estimate that out of every thousand cases of "naughtiness" among little children, nine hundred and ninety-nine are due to something else than a " bad " impulse in the child's heart. Old-wife wisdom has already reduced by one-half the percentage of infantile wickedness, in its fireside proverb, " Give a young one that's acting bad something to eat and put him to bed. Half the time he's tired or starved and don't know what ails him."

It now seems likely that the other half of the time he is either hungry for intellectual food, weary with the artificial stimulation of too much mingling with adult life, or exasperated by perfectly unnecessary insistence on a code of rules which has really nothing to do with the question of right or wrong conduct. When it comes to choosing between really right and really wrong conduct, apparently the majority of the child's natural instincts are for the really right, as is shown by his real preference for the orderly, educating activity of the Children's Home over disorderly " naughtiness." Our business should be to see to it that he is given the choice.

CHAPTER XII

DIFFICULTIES IN THE WAY OF A UNIVERSAL ADOPTION OF THE MONTESSORI IDEAS

NOW, of course, it is infinitely easier in the first place to cry out to a child, "Oh, don't be so careless!" than to consider thus with painful care all the elements lacking in his training which make him heedless, and throughout years of conscientious effort to exercise the ingenuity necessary to supply those lacking elements. But serious-minded parents do not and should not expect to find life a flowery bed of ease, and it is my conviction that most of us will welcome with heartfelt joy any possible solution of our desperately pressing problems, even if it involves the process of oiling and setting in motion the little-used machinery of our brains.

I am opposed in this optimistic conviction by that small segment of the circle of my acquaintances composed of the doctors whom I happen to know personally. They take a gloomy view of the matter and tell me that their experience with human nature leads them to fear that the rules of moral and intellectual hygiene of childhood, of this new system, excellent though they are, will be observed with as little faithfulness as the equally wise rules of physical hygiene for adults which the doctors have been endeavoring vainly to have us adopt. They inform me that they have learned that, if obedience to the laws of hygiene requires continuous effort, day after day, people will not obey them, even though by so doing they would avoid the pains and maladies which they so dread. " People will take pills," physicians report, " but they will not take exercise. If your new system told them of some one or two supreme actions which would benefit their children, quite a number of parents would strain every nerve to accomplish the necessary feats. But what you are telling them is only another form of what we cry so vainly, namely that they themselves must observe nature and follow her laws, and that no action of their doctors, wise though they may be, can vicariously perform this function for them. You will see that your Dr. Montessori's exhortations will have as little effect as those of any other physician."

I confess that at first I was somewhat cast down by these pessimistic prophecies, for even a casual glance over any group of ordinary acquaintances shows only too much ground for such conclusions. But a more prolonged scrutiny of just such a casually selected group of acquaintances, and a little more searching inquiry into the matter has brought out facts which lead to more encouraging ideas.

In the first place, the doctors are scarcely correct when they assume that they have always been the repository of a wisdom which we laity have obstinately refused to take over from them. Comparatively speaking, it is only yesterday that the doctors themselves outgrew the idea that pills were the divinely appointed cures for all ills. So recent is this revolution in ideas that there are still left among us in eddies, out of the main stream, elderly doctors who lay very little of the modern fanatical stress on diet, and burn very little incense before the modern altar of fresh air and exercise. It seems early in the day to conclude that the majority of mankind will not take good advice if it is offered them, a sardonic conclusion disproved by the athletic clubs all over the country, the sleeping-porches burgeoning out from large and small houses, the millions of barefooted children in rompers, the regiments of tennis-playing adolescents and golf-playing elders, the myriads of diet-studying housewives, the gladly accepted army of trained nurses. We may not do as well as we might, but we certainly have not turned deaf ears to all the exhortations of reason and enlightenment.

Furthermore, beside the fact that doctors have been preaching " hygiene against drugs " to us only a short time, it is to be borne in mind that, as a class, they do not add to their many noble and glorious qualities of mind and heart a very ardent proselytizing fervor. It seems to be against the " temperament " of the profession. If you go to a doctor's office, and consult him professionally he will, it is true, tell you nowadays not to take pills, but to take plenty of exercise and sleep, to eat moderately, avoid worry, and drink plenty of pure water; but you do not ever run across him preaching these doctrines from a barrel-head on the street-corner, to all who will hear. The traditional dignity of his profession forbids such Salvation Army methods. The doctors of a town are apt, prudently, to boil the water used in their own households and to advise this course of action to any who seek their counsel, rather than to band together in an aggressive, united company and make themselves disagreeably conspicuous by clamoring insistently at the primaries and polls for better water for the town. It is perhaps not quite fair to accuse us laity of obstinacy in refusing advice which has been offered with such gentlemanly reserve.

Then, there is the obvious fact that doctors, like lawyers, see professionally only the ailing or malcontents of the human family, and they suffer from a tendency common to us all, to generalize from the results of their own observation. Our own observation of our own community may quite honestly lead us to the opposite of their conclusions, namely that it is well worth while to make every effort for the diffusion of theories which tend to improve daily life, since, on the whole, people seem to have picked up very quickly indeed the reasonable doctrine of the prevention of illness by means of healthy lives. If they have done this, and are, to all appearances, trying hard to learn more about the process, it is reasonable to hope that they will catch at a similar reasonable mental and moral hygiene for their children, and that they will learn to leave off the unnecessary

mental and moral restrictions, the unwise interference
with the child's growth and undue insistence on con-
formity to adult ideas of regularity, just as they
have learned how to leave off the innumerable layers
of starched petticoats, the stiff scratchy pantalets,
and the close, smothering sunbonnets in which our loving and devoted great-grandmothers required our
grandmothers to grow up.

Lastly, there is a vital element in the situation
which is perhaps not sufficiently considered by people anxious to avoid the charge of sentimentality.
This element is the strength of parental affection,
perhaps the strongest and most enduring passion
which falls to the lot of ordinary human beings.
Only a Napoleon can carry ambition to the intensity
of a passion. Great, overmastering love between man
and woman is not so common as our romantic tradition would have us believe. In the world of religion,
saints are few and far between. Most of us manage
to live without being consumed by the reforming
fever of those rare souls who suffer under injustice
to others as though it were practised on themselves.
But nearly every house which contains children, shel-
ters also two human beings the hard crust of whose
natural egotism and moral sloth has been at least
cracked by the shattering force of this primeval passion for their young, two human beings, who, no matter how low their position in the scale of human
ethical development, have in them to some extent
that divine capacity for willing self-sacrifice which

comes, under other conditions, only to the rarest and most spiritual-minded members of the race. It is not sentimentality but a simple statement of fact to say that there is in parents who take care of their own children (as most American parents do) a natural fund of energy, patience, and willingness to undergo self-discipline, which cannot be counted upon in any other numerous class of people. The Montessori system, with its fresh, vivid presentation of axiomatic truths, with a fervent hope of a practical application of them to the everyday life of every child, addresses itself to these qualities in parents; and, for the sound development of its fundamental idea of self-education and self-government, trusts not only to the wise conclaves of professional pedagogues, but to the co-operation of the fathers and mothers of the world.

CHAPTER XIII

IS THERE ANY REAL DIFFERENCE BETWEEN THE MONTESSORI SYSTEM AND THE KINDERGARTEN?

NO one realizes more acutely than I that the composition of this chapter presupposes an amount of courage on my part which it is perhaps hardly exaggeration to call foolhardiness. That I am really venturing upon a battleground is evident to me from the note of rather fierce anticipatory disapproval which I hear in the voice of everyone who asks me the question which heads this chapter. It always accented, "*Is* there any real difference between the Montessori system and the kindergarten?" with the evident design of forcing a negative answer.

Oddly enough, the same reluctance to grant the possibility of anything new in the Italian method characterizes the attitude of those who intensely dislike the kindergartens, as well as that of its devoted adherents. People who consider the kindergarten " all sentimental, enervating twaddle " ask the question with a truculent tone which makes their query mean, " This new system is just the same sort of nonsense, isn't it now? "; while those who feel that the kindergarten is one of the vital, purifying, and uplifting forces in modern society evidently use the question as a means of stating, " It can't be anything different from the best kindergarten ideas, for they are the best possible."

I have seen too much beautiful kindergarten work and have too sincere an affection for the sweet and pure character of Froebel to have much community of feeling with the rather brutal negations of the first class of inquirers. If they can see nothing in kindergartens but the sentimentality which is undoubtedly there, but which cannot possibly, even in the most exaggerated manifestations of it, vitiate all the finely uplifting elements in those institutions, it is of no use to expect from them an understanding of a system which, like the Froebelian, rests ultimately upon a religious faith in the strength of the instinct for perfection in the human race.

It is therefore largely for the sake of people like myself, with a natural sympathy for the kindergarten, that I am setting out upon the difficult undertaking of stating what in my mind are the differences between a Froebelian and a Montessori school for infants.

I must begin by saying that there are a great many resemblances, as is inevitable in the case of two methods which work upon the same material— children from three to six. And of course it is hardly necessary formally to admit that the ultimate aim of the two educators is alike, because the aim which is common to them—an ardent desire to do the best thing possible for the children without regard for the convenience of the adults who teach them—is the sign manual throughout all the ages, from Plato and Quintilian down, which distinguishes the educator from the mere school-teacher.

There are a good many differences in the didactic apparatus and use of it, some of which are too technical to be treated fully here, such as the fact that Froebel, moved by his own extreme interest in crystals and their forms, provides a number of exercises for teaching children the analysis of geometrical forms, whereas Dr. Montessori thinks best not to undertake this with children so young. Kindergarten children are not taught reading and writing, and Montessori children are.   Kindergarten children learn more about the relations of wholes to parts in their " number work," while in the Casa dei Bambini there is more attention paid to numbers in their series.

There are of course many other differences in technic and apparatus, such as might be expected in two systems founded by educators separated from each other by the passage of sixty years and by a difference in race as well as by training and environment.   This is especially true in regard to the greater emphasis laid by Dr. Montessori on the careful, minute observation of the children before and during any attempt to instruct them.   Trained as she has been in the severely unrelenting rule for exactitude of the positive sciences, in which intelligent observation is elevated to the position of the cardinal virtue necessary to intellectual salvation, her instinct, strengthened since then by much experience, was to give herself plenty of time always to examine the subject of her experimentation. Just as a scientific horticulturist observes minutely the habits of a plant before he tries a new fertilizer on it, and after he has made the experiment goes on observing the plant with even more passionately absorbed attention, so Dr. Montessori trains her teachers to take time, all they need, to observe the children before, during, and after any given exercise. This is, of course, the natural instinct of Froebel, of every born teacher, but the routine of the average school or kindergarten gives the teacher only too few minutes for it, not to speak of the long hours necessary.

On the other hand, even in the details of the technic, there is much similarity between the two systems. Some of the kindergarten blocks are used in Montessori " sensory exercises." In both institutions the ideal, seldom attained as yet, is for the systematic introduction of gardening and the care of animals. In both the children play games and dance to music; some regular kindergarten games are used in the Casa dei Bambini; in both schools the first aim is to make the children happy; in neither are they reproved or punished. Both systems bear in every detail the imprint of extreme love and reverence for childhood. And yet the moral atmosphere of a kindergarten is as different from that of a Casa dei Bambini as possible, and the real

truth of the matter is that one is actually and fundamentally opposed to the other.

To explain this, a few words of comment on
Froebel, his life, and the subsequent fortunes of
his ideas may be useful. These facts are so well
known, owing to the universal respect and affection
for this great benefactor of childhood, that the
merest mention of them will suffice. The dates of
his birth and death are significant, 1782-1852, as
is a brief bringing to mind of the intensely German
Protestant piety of his surroundings. He died sixty
years ago, and a great deal of educational water has
flowed under school bridges since then. He died before anyone dreamed of modern scientific laboratories, such as those in which the Italian educator
received her sound, practical training, a training
which not only put at her disposition an amount of
accurate information about the subject of her investigation which would have dazzled Froebel, but
formed her in the fixed habit of inductive reasoning
which has made possible the brilliant achievements of
modern positive sciences, and which was as little common in Froebel's time as the data on which it works.
That he felt instinctively the needs for this solid
foundation is shown by his craving for instruction
in the natural sciences, his absorption of all the
scanty information within his reach, his subsequent
deep meditation upon this information, and his attempts to generalize from it.

Another factor in Froebel's life which scarcely

exists nowadays was the tradition of physical violence and oppression towards children. That this has gradually disappeared from the ordinary civilized family, is partly due to the general trend away from physical oppression of all sorts, and partly to Froebel's own softening influence, for which we can none of us feel too fervent a gratitude. He was forced to devote considerable of his energy to combating this tendency, which was not a factor at all in the problems which confronted Dr. Montessori.

Some time after his death his ideas began to spread abroad not only in Europe (the kindergartens of which I know nothing about, except that they are very successful and numerous), but also in the United States, about whose numerous and successful kindergartens we all know a great deal. The new system was taken up by teachers who were intensely American, and hence strongly characterized by the American quality of force of individuality. It is a universally accepted description of American women (sometimes intended as a compliment, sometimes as quite the reverse) that, whatever else they are, they are less negative, more forceful, more direct, endowed with more positive personalities than the women of other countries. These women, full of energy, quivering with the resolution to put into full practice all the ideas of the German educator whose system they espoused, " organized a campaign for kindergartens " which, with characteristic thoroughness, determination, and devotion, they have carried through to high success.

They, and the educators among men who became interested in the Froebelian ideas, have been by no means willing to consider all advance impossible because the founder of the system is no longer with them. They have been progressively and intelligently unwilling to let 1852 mark the culmination of kindergarten improvement, and they have changed, and patched, and added to, and taken away from the original method as their best judgment and the increasing scientific data about children enabled them. This process, it goes without saying, has not taken place without a certain amount of friction. Naturally everyone's " best judgment " scarcely coincided with that of everyone else. There have been honest differences of opinion about the interpretation of scientific data. True to its nature as an essentially religious institution, the kindergarten has undergone schisms, been rent with heresies, has been divided into orthodox and heterodox, into liberals and conservatives, although the whole body of the work has gone constantly forward, keeping pace with the increasing modern preoccupation with childhood.

Indeed it seems to me that one may say without being considered unsympathetic that it has now certain other aspects of a popular, prosperous religious sect, among which is a feeling of instinctive jealousy of similar regenerating influences which have their origin outside the walls of the original orthodox church.

Undoubtedly they have some excuse in the absurdly exaggerated current reports and rumors of the miracles accomplished by the Montessori apparatus; but it seems to outsiders that what we have a right to expect from the heads of the organized, established kindergarten movement is an open-minded, unbiased, and extremely minute and thorough investigation into the new ideas, rather than an inspection of popular reports and a resultant condemnation. It is because I am as much concerned as I am astonished at this attitude on their part that I am venturing upon the following slight and unprofessional discussion of the differences between the typical kindergarten and the typical Casa dei Bambini.

To begin with, kindergarteners are quite right when they cry out that there is nothing new in the idea of self-education, and that Froebel stated as plainly as Montessori does that the aim of all education is to waken voluntary action in the child. For that matter, what educator worthy of the name has not felt this? The point seems to be, not that Froebel states this vital principle any less clearly, but so much less forcibly than the Italian educator. Not foreseeing the masterful women, with highly developed personalities, who were to be the apostles of his ideas in America, and not being surrounded by the insistence on the value of each individuality which marks our modern moral atmosphere, it did not occur to him, apparently, that there was any special danger in this direction. For, of course, our modern high estimate of the value of individuality results not only in a vague though growing realization of the importance of safeguarding the nascent personalities of children, but in a plenitude of strongly marked individualities among the adults who teach children, and in a fixed habit of using the strength of this personality as a tool to attain desired ends.

The difference in this regard between the two educators may perhaps be stated fancifully in the following way: Froebel gives his teachers, among many other maxims to hang up where they may be constantly in view, a statement running somewhat in this fashion: "All growth must come from a voluntary action of the child himself." Dr. Montessori not only puts this maxim first and foremost, and exhorts her teachers to bear it incessantly in mind during the consideration of any and all other maxims, but she may be supposed to wish it printed thus: " All growth must come from a VOLUNTARY action of the child HIMSELF."

The first thing she requires of a directress in her school is a complete avoidance of the center of the stage, a self-annihilation, the very desirability (not to mention the possibility) of which has never occurred to the kindergarten teacher whose normal position is in the middle of a ring of children with every eye on her, with every sensitive, budding personality receiving the strongest possible impressions from her own adult individuality. Without the least hesitation or doubt, she has always considered that her part is to make that individuality as perfect and lovable as possible, so that the impression the children get from it may be desirable. The idea that she is to keep herself strictly in the background for fear of unduly influencing some childish soul which has not yet found itself, is an idea totally unheard of.

I find in a catalogue of kindergarten material this sentence in praise of some new device. " It obviates the need of supervision on the part of the teacher *as far as is consistent with conscientious child-training.*" Now the Montessori ideal is a device which shall be so entirely self-corrective that absolutely no interference by the teacher is necessary as long as the child is occupied with it. I find in that sentence the keynote of the difference between the two systems. In the kindergarten the emphasis is laid, consciously, or unconsciously, but very practically always, on the fact that the teacher teaches. In the Casa dei Bambini the emphasis is all on the fact that the child learns.

In the beginning of her study the kindergarten teacher is instructed, it is true, as a philosophic consideration, that Pestalozzi held and Froebel accepted the dictum that, just as the cultivator creates nothing in his trees and plants, so the educator creates nothing in the children under his care. This is duly set down in her note-book, but the apparatus given her to work with, the technic taught her, what she sees of the work of other teachers, the whole tendency of her training goes to accentuate what is already racially strong in her temperament, a fixed conviction of her own personal and individual responsibility for what happens about her. She feels keenly (in the case of nervous constitutions, crushingly) the weight of this responsibility, really awful when it is felt about children. She has the quick, energetic, American instinct to *do* something herself, at once to bring about a desired condition. She is the swimmer who does not trust heartily and wholly to the water to keep him up, but who stiffens his muscles and exhausts himself in the attempt by his own efforts to float. Indeed, that she should be required above all things to do nothing, not to interfere, is almost intellectually inconceivable to her.

This, of course, is a generalization as inaccurate as all generalizations are. There are some kindergarten teachers with great natural gifts of spiritual divination, strengthened by the experiences of their beautiful lives, who feel the inner trust in life which is so consoling and uplifting to the Montessori teacher. But the average American kindergarten teacher, like all the rest of us average Americans, needs the calming and quieting lesson taught by the great Italian educator's reverent awe for the spontaneous, ever-upward, irresistible thrust of the miraculous principle of growth.

In spite of the horticultural name of her school

the ordinary kindergarten teacher has never learned the whole-hearted, patient faith in the long, slow processes of nature which characterizes the true gardener. She is not penetrated by the realization of the vastness of the forces of the human soul, she is not subdued and consoled by a calm certainty of the rightness of natural development. She is far gayer with her children than the Montessori teacher, but she is really less happy with them because, in her heart of hearts, she trusts them less. She feels a restless sense of responsibility for each action of each child. It is doubtless this difference in mental attitude which accounts for the physical difference of aspect between our pretty, smiling, ever-active, always beckoning, nervously conscientious kindergarten teacher, always on exhibition, and the calm, unhurried tranquillity of the Montessori directress, always unobtrusively in the background.

The latter is but moving about from one little river of life to another, lifting a sluice gate here for a sluggish nature, constructing a dam there to help a too impetuous nature to concentrate its forces, and much of the time occupied in quietly observing, quite at her leisure, the direction of the channels being constructed by the different streams. The kindergarten teacher tries to do this, but she seems obsessed with the idea, unconscious for the most part, that it is, after all, her duty to manage somehow to increase the flow of the little rivers by pouring into them some of her own superabundant

vital force. In her commendable desire to give herself and her whole life to her chosen work, she con-
ceives that she is lazy if she ever allows herself
a moment of absolute leisure, and unoccupied, impersonal observation of the growth of the various
organisms in her garden. She must be always helping them grow! Why else is she there? she demands
with a wrinkled brow of nervous determination to
do her duty, and with the most honest, hurt surprise
at any criticism of her work.

It is possible that this tendency in American kindergartens is not only a result of the American
temperament, but is inherent in Froebel's original
conception of the kindergarten as the place where
the child gets his real social training, as opposed to
the home where he gets his individual training.
Standing midway between Fichte with his hard dictum that the child belongs wholly to the State and
to society, and Pestalozzi's conviction that he belongs wholly to the family, Froebel thought to make
a working compromise by dividing up the bone of
contention, by leaving the child in the family most
of the time, but giving him definite social training
at definite hours every day.

Now there is bound to be, in such an effort, some
of the same danger involved in a conception of
religious life which ordains that it shall be lived
chiefly between half-past ten and noon on every
Sunday morning. It may very well happen that a
child does not feel social some morning between nine

and eleven, but would prefer to pursue some laudable individual enterprise. It may be said that the slight moral coercion involved in insisting that he join in one of the group games or songs of the kindergarten is only good discipline, but the fact remains that coercion has been employed, even though coated with sweet and coaxing persuasion, and the picture of itself conceived by the kindergarten as a place of the spontaneous flowering of the social instinct among children has in it some slight pretense. In the Casa dei Bambini, on the other hand, the children learn the rules and conditions of social life as we must all learn them, and in the only way we all learn them, and that is by *living socially.*

The kindergarten teacher, set the task of seeing that a given number of children engage in social enterprises practically all the time during a given number of hours every day, can hardly be blamed if she is convinced that she must act upon the children nearly every moment, since she is required to round them up incessantly into the social corral. The long hours of the Montessori school and the freedom of the children, living their own everyday lives as though they were (as indeed they are) in their own home, make a vital difference here. The children, in conducting their individual lives in company with others, are reproducing the actual conditions which govern social life in the adult world. They learn to defer to each other, to obey rules, even to rise to the moral height of making rules, to sink temporarily their own interests in the common weal, not because it is "nice" to do this, not because an adored, infallible, lovely teacher supports the doctrine by her unquestioned authority, not because they are praised and petted when they do, but (and is not this the real grim foundation of laws for social organization?) because they find they cannot live together at all without rules which all respect and obey.

In other words, when there is some real occasion for formulating or obeying a law which facilitates social life, they formulate it and obey it from an inward conviction, based on genuine circumstances of their own lives, that they must do so, or life would not be tolerable for any of them; and when there is no genuine occasion for their making this really great sacrifice for the common weal, they are left, as we all desire to be left, to the pursuit of their own lives. No artificial occasion for this sacrifice is manufactured by the routine of the school—an artificial occasion which is apt to be resented by the stronger spirits among children even as young as those of kindergarten age. They feel, as we all do, that there is nothing intrinsically sacred or valuable about the compromises necessary to attain peaceable social life, and that they should not be demanded of us except when necessary. Crudely stated, Froebel's purpose seems to have been that the child should, in two or three hours at a given time every day, do his social living and have it over with. And although this statement is both unsympathetic and incomplete, there is in it the germ of a well-founded criticism of the method which many of us have vaguely felt, although we have not been able to formulate it before studying the principles of a system which seems to avoid this fault.

A conversation I had in Rome with an Italian friend, not in sympathy with the Montessori ideas, illustrates another phase of the difference between the average kindergarten and the Casa dei Bambini. My friend is a quick, energetic, positive woman who " manages " her two children with a competent ease which seems the most conclusive proof to her that her methods need no improvement. " Oh, no, the Case dei Bambini are quite failures," she told me. " The children themselves don't like them." I recalled the room full of blissful babies which I had come to know so well, and looked, I daresay, some of the amused incredulity I felt, for she went on hastily, " Well, *some* children may. Mine never did. I had to put both the boy and the girl back into a kindergarten. My little Ida summed up the whole matter. She said, ' Isn't it queer how they treat you at a Casa dei Bambini! They ask me, " Now which would you like to do, Ida, this, or this? " It makes me feel so queer. I want somebody to *tell* me what to do! ' "

My friend went on to generalize, quite sure of her ground, " That's the sweet and natural child instinct—to depend on adults for guidance. That's how children *are*, and all the Dr. Montessoris in the world can't change them."

The difference between that point of view and Dr. Montessori's is the fundamental difference between the belief in aristocracy, and the value of authority for its own sake, which still lingers among conservatives even in our day, and the whole-hearted belief in democracy which is growing more and more pronounced among most of our thinkers.

Ida is being trained under her mother's masterful eye to carry on docilely what an English writer has called " the dogmatic method with its demand for mechanical obedience and its pursuit of external results." She is acquiring rapidly the habit of standing still until somebody tells her what to do, and she has already acquired an unquestioning acquiescence in the illimitable authority of somebody else, anyone who will speak positively enough to regulate her life in all its details. In other words, a finely consistent little slave is being manufactured out of Ida, and if in later years she should develop more of her mother's forcefulness, it will waste a great deal of its energy in a wild, unregulated revolt against the chains of habit with which she finds herself loaded, and in the end will probably wreak itself on crushing the individuality out of her children in their turn.

Sweet little four-year-old Ida, freed for a moment from the twilight cell of her passive obedience, and blinking pitifully in the free daylight of the

Casa dei Bambini, is a figure which has lingered long in my memory and has been one of the factors inducing me to undertake the perhaps too ambitious enterprise of writing this book.

In still another way the Montessori insistence on spontaneity of the children's action safeguards them, it seems to me, against one of the greatest dangers of kindergarten life, and obviates one of the justest criticisms of the American development of Froebel's method, namely overstimulation and mental fatigue. When I first thoroughly grasped this fundamental difference, I was reminded of the saying of a wise old doctor who, when I was an intense, violently active girl of seventeen, had given me some sound advice about how to lift the little children with whom I happened to be playing: " Don't take hold of their hands to swing them around! " he cried to me. " You can't tell when the strain may be too great for their little bones and tendons. You may do them a serious hurt. Have them take hold of your hands! And when they're tired, they'll let go."

It now seems to me that in the kindergarten the teachers are the ones who take hold of the children's hands, and in the Casa dei Bambini it is the other way about. What Dr. Montessori is always crying to her teachers is just the exhortation of my old doctor. What she is endeavoring to contrive is a system which allows the children to " let go " when they themselves, each at a different time, feel the strain of effort. The kindergarten teacher is making

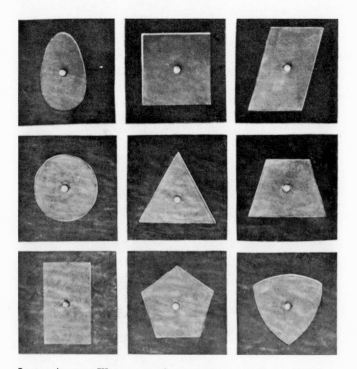

Insets Around Which the Child Draws, and Then Fills in
the Outline With Colored Crayons.

all possible conscientious efforts to train herself to an impossible achievement, namely to know (what of course she never can know with certainty) when each child loses his spontaneous interest in his exercises or game. She is as genuinely convinced as the Montessori directress that she must " let go " at that moment, but she is not trained so to take hold of the child that he himself makes that all-important decision.

It is true that the best kindergarteners learn from years of experience (which involves making mistakes on a good many children) about when, in general, to let go; but not the most inspired teacher can tell, as the child himself does, when the strain is first felt in the immature, undeveloped brain. And it is this margin of possibility of mistake on the part of the best kindergarten teachers which results only too frequently, with our nervous, too responsive American children, in the flushed faces and unnaturally bright eyes of the little ones who return to us after their happy, happy morning in the kindergarten, unable to eat their luncheons, unable to take their afternoon naps, quivering between laughter and tears, and finding very dull the quiet peace of the home life.

This observation finds any amount of confirmatory evidence in the astonishingly great diversity in mental application among children when really left to their own devices. There is no telling how long or how short a time any given play or game will hold their attention, and both kindergarteners and Montessori teachers agree that it is of value only so long as it really does genuinely hold their attention. Some children are interested only so long as they must struggle against obstacles, and once the enterprise runs smoothly, have no further use for it. With others, the pleasure seems to increase a hundredfold when they are once sure of their own ability.

For it is by no means true that the kindergarten teacher is always apt to continue a given game or exercise too long. It is only too long for some of the children. There are apt to be others whom she deprives, by her discontinuation of the game, of an invigorating exercise which they crave with all their might, and which they would continue, if left free to follow their own inclination, ten times longer than she would dare to think of asking them to do. The pertinacity of children in some exercise which happens exactly to suit their needs is one of the inevitable surprises to people observing them carefully for the first time. Since my attention has been called to it, I have observed this crazy perseverance on unexpected occasions in all children acting freely. Not long ago a child of mine conceived the idea of climbing up on an easy-chair, tilting herself over the arm, sliding down into the seat on her head, and so off in a sprawling heap on the floor. I began to count the number of times she went through this extremely violent, fatiguing, and (as far as I could see) uninteresting exercise, and was fairly astounded by her obstinacy in sticking to it. She had done it thirty-four times with unflagging zest, shouting and laughing to herself, and was apparently going on indefinitely when, to my involuntary relief, she was called away to supper.

In Rome I remember watching a little boy going through the exercises with the wooden cylinders of different sizes which fit into corresponding holes (page 70). He worked away with a busy, serene, absorbed industry, running his forefinger around the cylinders and then around the holes until he had them all fitted in. Then with no haste, but with no hesitation, he emptied them all out and began over again. He did this so many times that I felt an impatient fatigue at the sight of the laborious little creature, and turned my attention elsewhere. I had counted up to the fourteenth repetition of his feat before I stopped watching him, and when I glanced back again, a quarter of an hour later, he was still at it. All this, of course, without a particle of that " minimum amount of supervision consistent with conscientious child-training." He was his own supervisor, thanks to the self-corrective nature of the apparatus he was using. If he put a cylinder in the wrong hole he discovered it himself and was forced to think out for himself what the trouble was.

Dr. Montessori says (and I can easily believe her from my own experience) that nothing is harder for

even the most earnest and gifted teachers to learn
than that their duty is not to solve all the difficulties
in the way of the children, or even to smooth these
out as much as possible, but on the contrary expressly to see to it that each child is kept constantly
supplied with difficulties and obstacles suitable to
his strength.

A kindergarten teacher tries faithfully to teach
her children so that they will not make errors in their
undertakings.   She holds herself virtually responsible for this.   With a Puritan conscientiousness she
blames herself if they do make mistakes, if they do
not understand, by grasping her explanation, all the
inwardness of the process under consideration, and
she repeats her explanations with unending patience
until she thinks they do.   The Montessori teacher,
on the other hand, confines herself to pointing out
to the child what the enterprise before him is.   She
does not, it is true, drop down before him the material
for the Long Stair and leave him to guess what is
to be done with it.   She herself constructs the edifice
which is the goal desired.   She makes sure that he
has a clear concept of what the task is, and then
she mixes up the blocks and leaves him to work out
his own salvation by the aid of the self-corrective
material.

Dr. Montessori has a great many amusing stories
to tell of her first struggles with her teachers to
make them realize her point of view.   Some of them
became offended, and resolved, since they were not

allowed to help the children, to do nothing at all for
them, a resolution which resulted naturally in a state
of things worse than the first. It was very hard for
them to learn that it was their part to set the
machinery of an exercise in motion and then let the
child continue it himself. I quite appreciate the
difficulty of learning the distinction between directing the children's activity and teaching them each
new step of every process. My own impulse made
me realize the truth of Dr. Montessori's laughing
picture of the teacher's instinctive rush to the aid
of some child puzzling over the geometric insets, and
I knew, from having gone through many such pro-
fuse, voluble, vague, confusing explanations myself,
that what they always said was, "No, no, dear;
you're trying to put the round one in the square hole.
See, it has no corners. Look for a hole that hasn't
any corners, etc., etc." It was not until I had sat by
a child, restraining myself by a violent effort of self-
control from "correcting" his errors, and had seen
the calm, steady, untiring hopeful perseverance of his
application, untroubled and unconfused by adult
"aid," that I was fully convinced that my impulse
was to meddle, not to aid. And I admit that I have
many backslidings still.

Half playfully and half earnestly, I am continually quoting to myself the curious quatrain of the
Earl of Lytton, a verse which I think may serve as
a whimsical motto for all of us energetic American
mothers and kindergarteners who may be trying to

learn more self-restraint in our relations with little
children:

> " Since all that I can do for thee
> Is to do nothing, this my prayer must be,
> That thou mayst never guess nor ever see
> The all-endured, this nothing-done costs me."

CHAPTER XIV

MORAL TRAINING

A PERUSAL of the methods of the Montessori schools and of the philosophy underlying them may lead the reader to question if under this new system the child is regarded as a creature with muscular and intellectual activities only, and without a soul. While the sternest sort of moral training is given to the parent or teacher who attempts to use the Montessori system, apparently very little is addressed directly to the child.

Nothing could more horrify the founder of the system than such an idea. No modern thinker could possibly be more penetrated with reverence for the higher life of the spirit than she, or could bear its needs more constantly in mind.

Critics of the method who claim that it makes no direct appeal to the child's moral nature, and tends to make of him a little egotist bent on self-development only, have misapprehended the spirit of the whole system.

One answer to such a criticism is that conscious moral existence, the voluntary following of spiritual law, being by far the rarest, highest, and most difficult achievement in human life, is the one which develops latest, requires the longest and most careful preparation and the most mature powers of the individual. It is not only unreasonable to expect in a little child much of this conscious struggle toward the good, but it is utterly futile to attempt to force it prematurely into existence. It cannot be done, any more than a six-months baby can be forced to an intellectual undertaking of even the smallest dimension.

As a matter of fact, a normal child under six *is* mostly a little egotist bent on self-development, and to develop himself is the best thing he can do, both for himself and others, just as the natural business of a healthy child under a year of age is to extract all the physical profit possible out of the food, rest, care, and exercise given him. And yet even here, the line between the varieties of growth—physical, intellectual, and moral—is by no means hard and fast. The six-months baby, although living an almost exclusively physical life, in struggling to co-ordinate the muscles of his two arms so that he can seize a rattle with both hands, is battling for the mastery of his brain-centers, just as the three-year-old, who leads a life composed almost entirely of physical and intellectual interests, still, in the instinct which leads him to pity and water a thirsty plant, is struggling away from that exclusive imprisonment in his own interests and needs which is the Old Enemy of us all. The fact that this altruistic interest is not an overmastering passion which moves him to continuous responsible

care for the plant, and the other fact that, even while
he is giving it a drink, he has very likely forgotten
his original purpose in the fascinations of the antics
of water poured out of a sprinkling-pot, should not
in the least modify our recognition of the sincerely
moral character of his first impulse.

Now, sincerity in moral impulse is a prerequisite
to healthy moral life, the importance of which cannot be overstated by the most swelling devices of
rhetoric. It is an essential in moral life as air is in
physical life; in other words moral life of any kind
is entirely impossible without it. Hypocrisy, conscious or unconscious, is a far worse enemy than ignorance, since it poisons the very springs of spiritual
life, and yet few things are harder to avoid than unconscious hypocrisy. A realization of this truth is
perhaps the explanation of a recent tendency in
America for fairly intelligent, fairly conscientious
parents utterly to despair of seeing any light on
this problem, and to attempt to solve it by running
away from it, to throw up the whole business in dismay at its difficulty, to attempt no moral training
at all because so much that is given is bad, and to
"let the children go, until they are old enough to
choose for themselves."

It is possible that this method, chosen in desperation, bad though it obviously is, is better than
the older one of attempting to explain to little children the mysteries of the ordering of the universe before which our own mature spirits pause in bewildered

uncertainty. The children of six who conceive of
God as a policeman with a long white beard, oddly
enough placed in the sky, lying on the clouds, and
looking down through a peephole to spy upon the
actions of little girls and boys, have undoubtedly
been cruelly wronged by the creation of this grotesque and ignoble figure in their little brains, a
figure which, so permanent are the impressions of
childhood, will undoubtedly, in years to come, unconsciously render much more difficult a reverent and
spiritual attitude towards the Ultimate Cause. But
because this attempt at spiritual instruction is as
bad as it can be, it does not follow that the moral
nature of the little child does not need training fitted
to its capacities, limited though these undoubtedly are
in early childhood. There is no more reason for
leaving a child to grow up morally unaided by a life
definitely designed to develop his moral nature, than
for leaving him to grow up physically unaided by
good food, to expect that he will select this instinctively by his own unaided browsings in the pantry
among the different dishes prepared for the varying
needs of his elders.

The usual method by which bountiful Nature,
striving to make up for our deficiencies, provides for
this, is by the action of children upon each other.
This factor is, of course, notably present in the Casa
dei Bambini in the all-day life in common of twenty
children. In families it is especially to be seen in
the care and self-sacrifice which older children are

obliged to show towards younger ones. But in our usual small prosperous American families, this element of enforced moral effort is often wanting. Either there are but one or two children, or if more, the younger ones are cared for by a nurse, or by the mother sufficiently free from pressing material care to give considerable time to the baby of the family. And on the whole it must be admitted that Nature's expedient is at best a rough-and-ready one. Though the older children may miss an opportunity for spiritual discipline, it is manifestly better for the baby to be tended by an adult.

But there are other organisms besides babies which are weaker than children, and the care for plants and animals seems to be the natural door through which the little child may first go forth to his lifelong battle with his own egotism. It is always to be borne in mind that the Case dei Bambini now actually existing are by no means ideal embodiments of Dr. Montessori's ideas (see page 227). She has not had a perfectly free hand with any one of them and herself says constantly that many phases of her central principle have never been developed in practice. Hence the absence of any special morally educative element in the present Casa dei Bambini does not in the least indicate that Dr. Montessori has deliberately omitted it, any more than the perhaps too dryly practical character of life in the original Casa dei Bambini means anything but that the principle was being applied to very poor children who were in need, first

of all, of practical help. For instance, music and art
were left out of the life there, simply because, at that
time, there seemed no way of introducing them. It is
hard for us to realize that the whole movement is so
extremely recent that there has not been time to overcome many merely material obstacles. In the same
way, although circumstances have prevented Dr.
Montessori from developing practically the Casa dei
Bambini as far in the direction of the care of plants
and animals as she would like, she is very strongly
in favor of making this an integral and important
part of the daily life of little children.

In this she is again, as in so many of the features
of her system, only using the weight of her scientific
reputation to force upon our serious and respectful
attention means of education for little children which
have all along lain close at hand, which have been
mentioned by other educators (Froebel has, of course,
his elder boys undertake gardening), but of which,
as far as very young children go, our recognition
has been fitful and imperfect. She is the modern
doctor who proclaims with all the awe-compelling
paraphernalia of the pathological laboratory back
of him, that it is not medicine, but fresh air which is
the cure for tuberculosis. Most parents already make
some effort to provide pets (if they are not too much
trouble for the rest of the family) with a vague, instinctive idea that they are somehow "good for children," but with no conscious notion of how this
" good " is transferred or how to facilitate the proc-

ess ; and child-gardens are not only a feature of some
very advanced and modern schools and kindergartens,
but are provided once in a while by a family, although nearly always, as in Froebel's system, for
older children. But as those institutions are now conducted in the average family economy, the little child
gets about as casual and irregular an opportunity to
benefit by them as the consumptive of twenty years
ago by the occasional whiffs of fresh air which the
protecting care of his nurses could not prevent from
reaching him. The four-year-old, as he and his pets
are usually treated, *does not feel real responsibility*
for his kitten or his potted plant and, missing that,
he misses most of the good he might extract from his
relations with his little sisters of the vegetable and
animal world.

Our part, therefore, in this connection, is to catch
up the hint which the great Italian teacher has let
fall and use our own Yankee ingenuity in developing
it, always bearing religiously in mind the fundamental principle of self-education which must underlie
any attempt of ours to adapt her ideas to our conditions. For, of course, there is nothing new in the idea
of associating children with animals and plants—an
idea common to nearly all educators since the first
child played with a puppy. What is new is
our more conscious, sharpened, more definite idea,
awakened by Dr. Montessori's penetrating analysis,
of just how these natural elements of child-life
can be used to stimulate a righteous sense of re-

sponsibility. Our tolerant indifference towards the
children's dogs and cats and guinea-pigs, our fatigued complaint that it is more bother than it is
worth to prepare and oversee the handling of garden-
plots for the four- and five-year-olds, would be
transformed into the most genuine and ardent interest
in these matters, if we were penetrated with the realization that their purposeful use is the key to open
painlessly and naturally to our children the great
kingdom of self-abnegation. There is not, as is apt
to be the case with dolls, a more or less acknowledged
element of artificiality, even though it be the sweet
" pretend " mother-love for a baby doll. The children who really care for plants and animals are in a
sane world of reality, as much as we are in caring for
children. Their services are of real value to another
real life. The four-year-old youngster who rushes
as soon as he is awake to water a plant he had forgotten the day before, is acting on as genuine and
purifying an impulse of remorse and desire to make
amends as any we feel for a duty neglected in adult
life. The motives which underlie that most valuable
moral asset, responsibility, have been awakened, exercised, strengthened far more vitally than by any number of those Sunday morning "serious talks" in
which we may try fumblingly and futilely from the
outside to touch the child's barely nascent moral consciousness. The puppy who sprawls destructively
about the house, and the cat who is always under our
feet when we are in a hurry, should command respect-

ful treatment from us, since they are rehearsing quaintly with the child a first rough sketch of the drama of his moral life. The more gentleness, thoughtfulness, care, and forbearance the little child learns to show to this creature, weaker than himself, dependent on him, the less difficult he will find the exercise of those virtues in other circumstances. He is forming spontaneously, urged thereto by a natural good impulse of his heart, a moral habit as valuable to him and to those who are to live with him, as the intellectual habits of precision formed by the use of the geometric insets.

Of course, he will in the first place form this habit of unvarying gentleness towards plants and animals, only as he forms so many other habits, in simian imitation of the actions of those about him. He must absorb from example, as well as precept, the idea that plants and animals, being dependent on us, have a moral right to our unfailing care—a conception which is otherwise not suggested to him until he is several years older and has back of him the habit of several years of indifference toward this duty of the strong.

And so here is our hard-working Montessori parent embarked upon the career of animal-rearing, as well as child-training, with the added difficulty that he must care for the animals *through* the children, and resist stoutly the almost invincible temptation to take over this, like all other activities which belong by right to the child, for the short-cut reason that it is less trouble. If this impulse of the parent be followed, the mere furry presence will be of no avail to the child, except casually. The kitten must be the little girl's kitten if she is really to begin the long preparation which will lead her to the steady and resolute self-abnegations of maternity, the preparation which we hope will make her generation better mothers than we undisciplined and groping creatures are.

As for plant-life, the Antæus-like character of humanity is too well known to need comment. We are all healthier and saner and happier if we have not entirely severed our connection with the earth, and it is surprising that, recognizing this element as consciously as we do, we have made so comparatively little systematic and regular use of it in the family to benefit our little children. It is not because it is very hard to manage. What has been lacking has been some definite, understandable motive to make us act in this way, beyond the sentimental notion that it is pretty to have flowers and children together. No one before has told us quite so plainly and forcibly that this observation of plants and imaginative sympathy with their needs is the easiest and most natural way for little minds to get a first general notion of the world's economy, the struggle between helpful and hurtful forces, and of the duty of not remaining a passive onlooker at this strife, but of entering it instinctively, heartily throwing all one's powers on the side of the good and useful.

I know a child not yet quite three, who, by the maddeningly persistent interrogations characteristic of his age, has succeeded in extracting from a pair of gardening elders an explanation of the difference between weeds and flowers, and who has been so struck by this information that he has, entirely of his own volition, enlisted himself in the army of natural-born reformers. With the personal note of very little children, who find it so impossible to think in terms at all abstract, he has constructed in his baby mind an exciting drama in the garden, unfolding itself before his eyes; a drama in which he acts, by virtue of his comparatively huge size and giant strength, the generous rôle of *deus ex machina,* constantly rescuing beauty beset by her foes. He throws himself upon a weed, uproots it, and casts it away with the righteously indignant exclamation, "Horrid old weed! Stop eating the flowers' dinner!"

I do not think that it can be truthfully said that there are no moral elements in his life. He is a baby Sir Galahad, with roses for his maidens in distress. He has felt and exercised and strengthened the same impulse that drove Judge Lindsey to his battle for the children of Denver against the powers of graft. He has recognized spontaneously his duty to aid the good and useful against their enemies, the responsibility into which he was born when he opened his eyes upon the world of mingled good and evil.

All this is not a fanciful literary flight of the imagination. It is not sentimentality. It is calling things by their real names. Because the little child's capacity for a genuine moral impulse is small and has, like all his other capacities, little continuity, is no reason why we should not think clearly about it and recognize it for what it is—the key to the future. Because he " makes a play " of his good action and is not priggishly aware of his virtue is all the more reason for us to be thankful, for that is a proof of its unforced existence in his spirit. Just as the child " makes a play " out of his geometric insets, and is not pedantically aware that he is acquiring knowledge, so, to take an instance from the Casa dei Bambini, the little girls who set the tables and bring in the soup are only vastly interested in the fun of " playing waitress." It is their elders who perceive that they are unconsciously and painlessly acquiring the habit of willing and instinctive service to others, which will aid them in many a future conscious and painful struggle against their own natural selfishness and inertia.

This use of the sincerely common life in the Children's Home to promote sincerely social feeling among the children has been mentioned in the preceding chapter. It is one of the most vitally important of the elements in the Montessori schools. The genuine, unforced acceptance by the children of the need for sacrifices by the individual for the good of all, is something which can only be brought about by genuinely social life with their equals, such as they have in the Children's Home and not elsewhere. We must do the best we can in the family-life by seeing that the child shares as much as possible and as sincerely as possible in the life of the household. But at home he is inevitably living with his inferiors, plants, animals, and babies; or his superiors, older children and adults; whereas in the Children's Home he is living as he will during the rest of his life, mostly with his equals. And it is in the spontaneous adjustments and compromises of this continuous life with his equals that he learns most naturally, most soundly, and most thoroughly, the rules governing social life.

As for moral life, it seems to me that we need neither make a vain attempt to subscribe to a too-rosy belief in the unmixed goodness of human nature, and blind ourselves to the saddening fact that the battle against one's egotism is bound to be painful, nor, on the other hand, go back to the grim creed of our forefathers, that the sooner children are thrust into the thick of this unending war the better, since they must enter it sooner or later. The truth seems to lie in its usual position, between two extremes, and to be that children should be strengthened by proper moral food, care, and exercises suited to their strength, and allowed to grow slowly into adult endurance before they are forced to face adult moral problems; and that we may protect them from too great demands on their small fund of capacity for self-sacrifice by allowing them and even encouraging them to wreathe their imaginative " plays " about the self-sacrificing action, provided, of course, that we keep our heads clear to make sure that the " plays " do not interfere with the action.

It is well to make a plain statement to the child of five, that he is requested to wipe the silver-ware because it will be of service to his mother (if he is lucky enough to have a mother who ever does so obviously necessary and useful a thing as to wash the dishes herself), but it is not necessary to insist that this conception of service shall uncompromisingly occupy his mind during the whole process. It does no harm if, after this statement, it is suggested that the knives and forks and spoons are shipwrecked people in dire need of rescue, and that it would be fun to snatch them from their watery predicament and restore them safely to their expectant families in the silver-drawer. By so doing we are not really confusing the issue, or " fooling " the child into a good action, if clear thinking on the part of adults accompany the process. We are but suiting the burden to the childish shoulders, but inducing the child-feet to take a single step, which is all that any of us can take at one time, in the path leading to the service of others.

Most of this chapter has been drawn from Montessori ideas by inference only, by the development of hints, and it is probable that other mothers, meditating on the same problems, may see other ways of applying the principle of self-education and spontaneous activity to this field of moral life. It is apparent that the first element necessary, after a firm grasp on the fundamental idea that our children must do their own moral as well as physical growing, and after a vivid realization that the smallest amount of real moral life is better than much simulated and unreal feeling, is clear thinking on our part, a definite notion of what we really mean by moral life, a definition which will not be bounded and limited by the repetition of committed-to-memory prayers. This does not mean that simple nightly aspirations to be a good child the next day may not have a most beneficial effect on even a very young child and may satisfy the first stirrings to life of the religious instinct, as much as the constant daily kindnesses to plants and animals satisfy the ethical instinct. This latter, however, at his age, is apt to be vastly more developed and more important than the religious instinct.

Indeed the religious instinct, which apparently never develops in some natures, although so strong in others, is in all cases slow to show itself and, like other slowly germinating seeds, should not be pushed and prodded to hasten it, but should be left untouched until it shows signs of life. Our part is to prepare, cultivate, and enrich the nature in which it is to grow.

CHAPTER XV

DR. MONTESSORI'S LIFE AND THE ORIGIN OF THE CASA DEI BAMBINI

DR. MONTESSORI and the average American parent are as different in heredity, training, and environment as two civilized beings can very well be. Every condition surrounding the average American child is as materially different as possible from those about the children in the original Casa dei Bambini. Hence the usual sound rule that the individuality and personal history of the scientist do not concern the student of his work does not hold in this case. The conditions in Rome where Dr. Montessori has done her work, differ so entirely from those of ordinary American life, in the conduct of which we hope to profit by her experiments, that it is only fair to Americans interested in her work, to give them some notion of the varying influences which have shaped the career of this woman of genius.

This is so especially in her case, because, as a nation, we are more ignorant of modern Italian life than of that of any great European nation. Modern Italy, wrestling with all the problems of modern industrial and city life grafted upon an age-old civilization, endeavoring to enlighten itself, to take the

best from twentieth-century progress without losing its own individual virtues, this is a country as
unknown to us as the regions of the moon. And yet
to understand Dr. Montessori's work and the vicis-
situdes of her undertakings, we must have at least
a summary knowledge that the Italian world of to-
day is in a curious ferment of antiquated prejudices
and highly progressive thought.

To us, as a rule, Rome is " The Eternal City " of
our school-Latin days, whereas, in reality, it is, for
all practical purposes as a city, much more recent
than New York—about as old, let us say, as Detroit.
But Detroit planted its vigorously growing seedling
in the open ground and not in a cracked pot of small
dimensions. Hence the problems of the two modern cities are dissimilar. I heard it suggested by a
man of authority in the Italian government that
a great mistake had been made when the modern
capital of Italy had been dumped down upon the
heap of historic ruins which remained of ancient
Rome. It had been bad for the ruins and very hard
on the modern capital. If a site had been selected
just outside the walls of old Rome, a nineteenth-cen-
tury metropolis could have sprung up with the
effortless haste with which our own Middle Western
plains have produced cities. One thing is certain,
Dr. Montessori's Case dei Bambini would not have
taken their present form under other conditions, and
this is what concerns us here.

But before the origin of the Case dei Bambini is

taken up, a brief biography of their creator will help us to understand her development. Her early life, before her choice of a profession, need not interest us beyond the fact that she is the only child of devoted parents, not materially well-to-do. Now, as a result of a too-rapid social transformation among the Italians, the " middle class " population forms a much smaller proportion of the inhabitants of Italy than in other modern nations. One result of this condition is that the brilliant daughter of parents not well-to-do, finds it much harder to pass into a class of associates and to find an intellectual background which suits her nature, than a similarly intellectual and original American girl. Even now in Italy such a girl is forced to fight an unceasing battle against social prejudice and intellectual inertia. It can be imagined that when Dr. Montessori was the beautiful, gifted girl-student of whom older Romans speak with enthusiasm or horror, according to the centuries in which they morally live, her will-power and capacity for concentration must have been finely tempered in order not to break in the long struggle.

Judging by the talk one hears in Rome about the fine, youthful fervor of Dr. Montessori's early struggle against conditions hampering her mental and spiritual progress, she is a surviving pioneer of social frontier prejudice, who has emerged from the battle with pioneer conditions endowed with the hickory-like toughness of intellectual fiber of will and of character which is the reward of sturdy pioneers. Certain it is that her battles with prejudices of all sorts have hardened her intellectual muscles and trained her mental eye in the school of absolute moral self-dependence, that moral self-dependence which is the aim and end of her method of education and which will be, as rapidly as it can be realized, the solvent for many of our tragic and apparently insoluble modern problems.

It is hard for an American of this date to realize the bomb-shell it must have been to an Italian family a generation ago when its only daughter decided to study medicine. So rapidly have conditions surrounding women changed that there is no parallel possible to be made which could bring home to us fully the tremendous will-power necessary for an Italian woman of that time and class to stick to her resolution. The fangs of that particular prejudice have been so well-nigh universally drawn that it is safe to say that an American family would see its only daughter embark on the career of animal-tamer, steeple-jack, or worker in an iron foundry, with less trepidation than must have shadowed the early days of Dr. Montessori's medical studies. One's imagination can paint the picture from the fact that she was the first woman to obtain the degree of Doctor of Medicine, from the University of Rome, an achievement which was probably rendered none the easier by the fact that she was both singularly beautiful and singularly ardent.

After graduation she became attached, as assistant doctor, to the Psychiatric Clinic at Rome. At that time, one of the temporary expedients of self-modernizing Italy was to treat the idiot and feeble-minded children in connection with the really insane, a rough-and-ready classification which will serve vividly to illustrate the desperate condition of Italy of that date. The young medical graduate had taken up children's diseases as the " specialty " which no self-respecting modern doctor can be without, and naturally in her visits to the insane asylums (where the subjects of her Clinic lived), her attention was attracted to the deficient children so fortuitously lodged under the same roof.

I go into the details of the oblique manner in which she embarked upon the prodigious undertaking of education without any conscious knowledge of the port toward which she was directing her course, in order to bring out clearly the fact that she approached the field of pedagogy from an entirely new direction, with absolutely new aims and with a wholly different mental equipment from those of the technically pedagogical, philosophic, or social-reforming persons who have labored so conscientiously in that field for so many generations.

This young doctor, then, trained by hard knocks to do her own thinking and make her own decisions, found that her absorbed study of abnormal and deficient children led her straight along the path taken by the nerves from their unregulated external

activities to the brain-centers which rule them so
fitfully. The question was evidently of getting at
the brain-centers. Now the name of the process of
getting at brain-centers is one not usually encountered in the life of the surgeon. It is education.

The doctor at work on these problems was all the
time in active practice as a physician, an influence
in her life which is not to be forgotten in summing
up the elements which have formed her character. She
was performing operations in the hospitals, taking
charge of grave diseases in her private practice, ex-
posing herself to infection of all sorts in the in-
fectious wards of the hospitals, liable to be called up
at any hour of the night to attend a case anywhere
in the purlieus of Rome. It was a soldier tried and
tested in actual warfare in another part of the battle for the betterment of humanity, who finally took
up the question of the training of the young. She
parted company with many of her fellow-students of
deficient children, and faced squarely the results of
her reasoning. Not for her the position aloof, the
observation of phenomena from the detached standpoint of the distant specialist. If nervous diseases
of children, leading to deficient intellectual powers,
could be best attacked through education, the obvious
step was to become an educator.

She gave up her active practice as a physician
which had continued steadily throughout all her other
activities, and accepted the post of Director of the
State Orthophrenic School (what we would call an

Institute for the Feeble-Minded), and, throwing herself into the work, heart and soul, with all the ardor
of her race and her own temperament, she utilized
her finely-tempered brain and indomitable will, in
the hand-to-hand struggle for the actual amelioration of existing conditions. For years she taught the
children in the Asylum under her care, devoting herself to them throughout every one of their waking
hours, pouring into the poor, cracked vases of their
minds the full, rich flood of her own powerful in-
tellect. All day she worked with her children, loved
to idolatry by them, exhausting herself over their
problems like the simplest, most unthinking, most
unworldly, and devout sister of charity; but at night
she was the scientist again, arranging, classifying,
clarifying the results of the day's observation, examining with minute attention the work of all those
who had studied her problems before her, applying
and elaborating every hint of theirs, every clue discovered in her own experiments.

Those were good years, years before the world
had heard of her, years of undisturbed absorption
in her work.

Then, one day, as such things come, after long,
uncertain efforts, a miracle happened. A supposedly deficient child, trained by her methods,
passed the examinations of a public school with more
ease, with higher marks than normal children prepared in the old way. The miracle happened again
and again and then so often that it was no longer a

miracle, but a fact to be foretold and counted on with certainty.

Then the woman with the eager heart and trained mind drew a long breath and, determining to make this first success only the cornerstone of a new temple, turned to a larger field of action, the field to which her every unconscious step had been leading her, the education, no longer only of the deficient, but of all the normal young of the human race.

It was in 1900 that Dr. Montessori left the Scuola Ortofrenica, and began to prepare herself consciously and definitely for the task before her. For seven years she followed a course of self-imposed study, meditation, observation, and intense thought. She began by registering as a student of philosophy in the University of Rome and turned her attention to experimental psychology with especial reference to child-psychology. The habit of her scientific training disposed her naturally as an accompaniment to her own research to examine thoroughly the existing and recognized authorities in her new field. She began to visit the primary schools and to look about her at the orthodox and old-established institutions of the educational world with the fresh vision only possible to a mind trained by scientific research to abhor preconceived ideas and to come to a conclusion only after weighing actual evidence.

No more diverting picture can be imagined than the one presented by this keen-eyed, clear-headed

scientist surveying, with an astonishment which must
have been almost dramatically apparent, the rows
of immobile little children nailed to their stationary
seats and forced to give over their natural birth-
right of activity to a well-meaning, gesticulating,
explaining, always fatigued, and always talking
teacher. It was evident at a glance that she could
not find there what she had hoped to find, that first
prerequisite of the modern scientist, a prolonged
scrutiny of the natural habits of the subject of investigation. The entomologist seeking to solve some
of the farmer's problems, spends years with a micro-
scope, studying the habits of the potato and of the
potato-bug before he tries to invent a way to help
the one and circumvent the other. But Dr. Montessori found, so to speak, that all the potatoes she
tried to investigate were being grown in a cellar.
They grew, somehow, because the upward thrust of
life is invincible, but their pale shoots gave no evidence of the possibility of the sturdy stems, which
a chance specimen or two escaped by a stroke of
luck from the cellar, proved to be possible for the
whole species.

At the same time that she was making these
amazed and disconcerted visits to the primary
schools, she was devouring all the books which have
been written on her subject. My own acquaintance
with works on pedagogy is limited, but I observe
that people who do know them do not seem surprised
that this thoroughly trained modern doctor, with

years of practical teaching back of her, should have found little aid in them. Two highly valuable authorities she did find, significantly enough doctors like herself, one who lived at the time of the French Revolution and one perhaps fifty years later. She tells us in her book what their ideas were and how strongly they modified her own; but as we are here chiefly concerned with the net result of her thought, it would not be profitable to go exhaustively into the investigation of her sources. It is enough to say that most of us would never in our lives have heard of those two doctors if she had not studied them.

We have now followed the course of Dr. Montessori's life until it brings us back to that chaotic, ancient-modern Rome, mentioned a few paragraphs above, struggling with all sorts of modern problems of city life. The housing of the very poor is a question troublesome enough, even to Detroit or Indianapolis with their bright, new municipal machinery. In Rome the problem is complicated by the medieval standards of the poor themselves as to their own comfort; by the existence of many old rookeries where they may roost in unspeakable conditions of filth and promiscuity; and by the lack of a widespread popular enlightenment as to the progress of the best modern communities. But, though Italian public opinion as a whole seems to be in a somewhat dazed condition over the velocity of changes in the social structure, there is no country in the world which has more acute, powerful, or original intelligences and consciences trained on our modern problems. All the while that Dr. Montessori had been trying to understand the discrepancy between the rapid advance of idiot children under her system and the slow advance of normal children under old-fashioned methods, another Italian, an influential, intelligent, and patriotic Roman, Signor Edoardo Talamo, was studying the problem of bettering at once, practically, the housing of the very poor.

He had decided what to do and had done it, when the line of his activity and that of Dr. Montessori's met in one of those apparently fortuitous combinations of elements destined to form a compound which is exactly the medicine needed for some unhealthy part of the social tissue. The plan of Signor Talamo's model tenements was so wise and so admirably executed that, except for one factor, they really deserved their name. This factor was the existence of a large number of little children under the usual school age, who were left alone all day while their mothers, driven by the grinding necessity which is the rule in the Italian lower working classes, went out to help earn the family living. These little ones wandered about the clean halls and stairways, defacing everything they could reach and constantly getting into mischief, the desolating ingenuity of which can be imagined by any mother of small children. It was evident that the money taken to repair

the damage done by them would be better employed
in preventing them from doing it in the first place.
Signor Talamo conceived the simple plan of setting
apart a big room in every one of his tenement houses
where the children could be kept together. This, of
course, meant that some grown person must be there
to look after them.

Now Rome is, at least from the standpoint of a
New Yorker or a Chicagoan, a small city, where
"everyone who is anyone knows everyone else." Although the sphere of Signor Talamo's activity was
as far as possible from that of the pioneer woman
doctor specializing in children's brain-centers, he
knew of her existence and naturally enough asked
her to undertake the organization and the management of the different groups of children in his tenement houses, collected, as far as he was concerned,
for the purpose of keeping them from scratching
the walls and fouling the stairways.

On her part Dr. Montessori took a rapid mental
survey of these numerous groups of normal children at exactly the age when she thought them most
susceptible to the right sort of education, and saw
in them, as if sent by a merciful Providence, the
experimental laboratories which she so much needed
to carry on her work and which she had definitely found that primary schools could never become.

The fusion of two elements which are destined to
combine is not a long process once they are brought

together. How completely Dr. Montessori was prepared for the opportunity thus given her can be calculated by the fact that the first Casa dei Bambini was opened on the 6th of January, 1907, and that now, only five years after, there arrive in Rome, from every quarter of the globe, bewildered but imperious demands for enlightenment on the new idea.

For it was at once apparent that the fundamental principle of self-education, which had been growing larger and larger in Dr. Montessori's mind, was as brilliantly successful in actual practice as it was plausible in abstract thought. Evidently entire freedom for the children was not only better for the purposes of the scientific investigator, but infinitely the best thing for the children. All those meditations about the real nature of childhood, over which she had been brooding in the long years of her study, proved themselves, once put to the test, as axiomatic in reality as they had seemed. Her theories held water. The children justified all her visions of their capacity for perfectibility and very soon went far beyond anything even she had conceived of their ability to teach and to govern themselves. For instance, she had not the least idea, when she began, of teaching children under six how to write. She held, as most other educators did, that on the whole it was too difficult an undertaking for such little ones. It was her own peculiar characteristic, or rather the characteristic of her scientific training, of extreme openness to conviction which induced her, after practical

experience, to begin her famous experiments with
the method for writing.

The story of this startling revelation of unsus-
pected forces in human youth and of the almost
instant pounce upon it by the world, distracted by
a helpless sense of the futility and clumsiness of
present methods of education, is too well known to
need a long recapitulation. The first Casa dei Bambini was established in January, 1907, without at-
tracting the least attention from the public. About
a year after another one was opened. This time,
owing to the marked success of the first, the affair
was more of a ceremony, and Dr. Montessori delivered there that eloquent inaugural address which is
reprinted in the American translation of her book.
By April of 1908, only a little over a year after the
first small beginning, the institution of the Casa
dei Bambini was discovered by the public, keen on
the scent of anything that promised relief from
the almost intolerable lack of harmony between
modern education and modern needs. Pilgrims of
all nationalities and classes found their way through
the filthy streets of that wretched quarter, and the
barely established institution, still incomplete in many
ways, with many details untouched, with many others
provided for only in a makeshift manner, was set
under the microscopic scrutiny of innumerable sharp
eyes.

The result, as far as we are concerned, we all
know: the rumors, vague at first, which blew across

our lives, then more definite talk of something really new, then the characteristically American promptness of response in our magazines and the almost equally prompt appearance of an English translation of Dr. Montessori's book.

And, so far, that is all we have from her, and for the present it is all we can have, without taking some action ourselves to help her. It is a strange situation, intensely modern, which could only have occurred in this age of instantly tattling cables and telegrams. It is, of course, a great exaggeration to say that all educated parents and teachers in America are interested in the Montessori system, but the proportion who really seem to be, is astonishing in the extreme when one considers the very recent date of the beginning of the whole movement. Over there in Rome, in a tenement house, a woman doctor begins observations in an experimental laboratory of children, and in five years' time, which is nothing to a real scientist, her laboratory doors are stormed by inquirers from Australia, from Norway, from Mexico, and, most of all, from the United States. Teachers of district schools in the Carolinas write their cousins touring in Europe to be sure to go to Rome to see the Montessori schools. Mothers from Oregon and Maine write, addressing their letters, " Montessori, Rome," and make demands for enlightenment, urgent, pressing, peremptory, and shamelessly peremptory, since they conceive of a possibility that their children, their own children, the

WORD BUILDING WITH CUT-OUT ALPHABET.

most important human beings in the world, may be missing something valuable. From innumerable towns and cities, teachers, ambitious to be in the front of their profession, are taking their hoarded savings from the bank and starting to Rome with the naïve conviction that their own thirst for information is sufficient guarantee that someone will instantly be forthcoming to provide it for them.

When they reach Rome, most of them quite unable to express themselves in Italian or even in French, what do they find, all these tourists and letters of inquiry, and adventuring school-mistresses? They find a dead wall. They have an unformulated idea that they are probably going to a highly organized institution of some sort, like our huge " model schools " attached to our normal colleges, through the classrooms of which an unending file of observers is allowed to pass. And they have no idea whatever of the inevitability *with which Italians speak Italian.*

They find—if they are relentlessly persistent enough to pierce through the protection her friends try to throw about her—only Dr. Montessori herself, a private individual, phenomenally busy with very important work, who does not speak or understand a word of English, who has neither money, time, or strength enough single-handed to cope with the flood of inquiries and inquirers about her ideas. In order to devote herself entirely to the great undertaking of transmuting her divinations of the truth into a definite, logical, and scientific system, she has withdrawn herself more and more from public life. She has resigned from her chair of anthropology in the University of Rome, and last year sent a substitute to do her work in another academic position not connected with her present research—and this although she is far from being a woman of independent means. She has sacrificed everything in her private life in order to have, for the development of her educational ideas, that time and freedom so constantly infringed upon by the well-meaning urgency of our demands for instruction from her.

She lives now in the most intense retirement, never taking a vacation from her passionate absorption in her work, not even giving herself time for the exercise necessary for health, surrounded and aided by a little group of five devoted disciples, young Italian women who live with her, who call her " mother," and who exist in and for her and her ideas, as ardently and whole-heartedly as nuns about an adored Mother Superior. Together they are giving up their lives to the development of a complete educational system based on the fundamental idea of self-education which gave such brilliant results in the Casa dei Bambini with children from three to six. For the past year, helped spiritually by these disciples and materially by influential Italian friends, Dr. Montessori has been experimenting with the application of her ideas to children from six to nine, and I think it is no violation of her confidence to report that these experiments have been as astonishingly successful as her work with younger children.

It is to this woman burning with eagerness to do her work, absorbed in the exhausting problems of intellectual creation, that students from all over the world are turning for instruction in a phase of her achievement which now lies behind her. The woman in the genius is touched and heartened by the sudden homage of the world, but it is the spirit of the investigating scientist which most often inhabits that powerful, bulky, yet lightly poised body and looks out from those dark, prophetic eyes; and from the point of view of the scientist, the world asks too much when it demands from her that she give herself up to normal teaching. For it must be apparent from the sketch of her present position that she would need to give up her very life were she to accede to all the requests for training teachers in her primary method, since she is simply a private individual, has no connection with the official educational system of her country, is at the head of no normal school, gives no courses of lectures, and has no model schools of her own to which to invite visitors. It is hard to believe her sad yet unembittered statement that there is now in Rome not one primary school which is entirely under her care, which she authorizes in all its detail, which is really a "Montessori School." There are, it is true, some which she started and which are still conducted according to her ideas in the majority of details, but not one where she is the leading spirit.

There are a variety of reasons, natural enough when one has once taken in the situation, which account for this state of things, so bewildering and disconcerting to those who have come from so far to learn at headquarters about the new ideas. The Italian Government, straining to carry the heavy burdens of a modern State, feels itself unable to undertake a radical and necessarily very costly reorganization of its schools, the teachers very naturally fear revolutionary changes which would render useless their hard-won diplomas, and carry on against the new system a secret campaign which has been so far successful. Hence it happens that investigators coming from across seas have the not unfamiliar experience of finding the prophet by no means head of the official religion of his own country.

In the other camp, fighting just as bitterly, are the Montessori adherents, full of enthusiasm for her philosophy, devoting all the forces at their command (and they include many of the highest intellectual and social forces) to the success of the cause which they believe to be of the utmost importance to the future of the race. It can be seen that the situation is not orderly, calm, or in any way adapted to dispassionate investigation.

And yet people who have come from California and British Columbia and Buenos Ayres to seek for information, naturally do not wish to go back to their distant homes without making a violent effort to investigate. What they usually try to do is to force

from someone in authority a card of admission either
to the Montessori school held in the Franciscan
Nunnery on the Via Giusti, or to another conducted
by Signora Galli among the children of an extremely
poor quarter of Rome, or, innocent and unaware,
in all good faith go to visit the institutions in the
model tenements, still called Case dei Bambini. But
Dr. Montessori's relations with those schools ceased
in 1911 as a result of an unfortunate disagreement
between Signor Talamo and herself in which, so far
as an outsider can judge, she was not to blame; and
those infant schools are now thought by impartial
judges to be far from good expositions of her
methods, and in many cases are actual travesties of
it. Furthermore, Dr. Montessori has now no connection with Signora Galli's schools. This leaves
accessible to her care and guided by her counsels
only the school held in the Franciscan nunnery, which
is directed by Signorina Ballerini, one of Dr. Montessori's own disciples, as the nearest approach to
a school under her own control in Rome. This is,
in many ways, an admirable example of the wonderful result of the Montessori ideas and is a revelation
to all who visit it. But even here, though the good
nuns make every effort to give a free hand to
Signorina Ballerini, it can be imagined that the eccle-
siastical atmosphere, which in its very essence is
composed of unquestioning obedience to authority,
is not the most congenial one for the growth of a
system which uses every means possible to do away

with dogma of any sort, and to foster self-dependence and first-hand ideas of things. More than this, if this school admitted freely all those who wish to visit it, there would be more visitors than children on many a day.

It is not hard to sympathize with the searchers for information who come from the ends of the earth, who stand aghast at this futile ending of their long journey. And yet it would be the height of folly for the world to call away from her all-important work an investigator from whom we hope so much in the future. How can we expect her, against all manner of material odds, to organize a normal school in a country with a government indifferent, if not hostile to her ideas, to gather funds, to rent rooms, to arrange hours, hire janitors, and lay out courses!

But the proselytizer who lives in every ardent believer makes her as unreconciled to the state of things as we are. She is regretfully aware of the opportunity to spread the new gospel which is being lost with every day of silence, distressed at the thought of sending the pilgrims away empty-handed, and above all naturally distracted with anxiety lest impure, misunderstanding caricatures of her system spread abroad in the world as the only answer to the demand for information about it. Busy as she is with the most absorbing investigations, Dr. Montessori is willing to meet the world halfway. If those who ask her to teach them will do the tangible, comparatively simple work of establishing an Institute of Experimental Pedagogy in Rome, the Dottoressa, for all her concentration on her further research, will be more than willing to give enough of her time for making the school as wonderful, beautiful, and inspiring as only a Montessori school can be.

Our part should be to endeavor to learn from her what we can without disturbing too much that freedom of life which is as essential to her as to the children in her schools, to give generously to an Institute of Experimental Pedagogy, and then freely allow her own inspiration to shape its course. Surely the terms are not hard ones, and it is to be hoped that the United States, with the genuine, if somewhat haphazard, willingness to further the cause of education, which is perhaps our most creditable national characteristic, will accept the offered opportunity and divert a little of the money now being spent in America on scientific investigation of every sort to this investigation so vital for the coming generation. The need is urgent, the sum required is not large, the opportunity is one in a century, and the end to be gained valuable beyond the possibility of exaggeration, for, as Dr. Montessori quotes at the end of the preface of her book, " Whoso strives for the regeneration of education strives for the regeneration of the human race."

CHAPTER XVI

SOME LAST REMARKS

THAT there is little prospect of an immediate adoption in the United States of Montessori ideas of flexibility and unhampered individual growth is apparent to anyone who knows even slightly the hierarchic rigidity of our system of education with its inexorable advance along fixed foreordained lines, from the kindergarten through the primary school, on through the high school to the Chinese ordeal of the college entrance examination, an event which casts its shadow far down the line of school-grades, embittering the intellectual activities and darkening the life of teachers and pupils (even pupils who have not the faintest chance of going to college) for years before the awful moment arrives.

All really good teachers have always been, as much as they were allowed to be, some variety of what is called in this book " Montessori teacher." But as the State and private systems of education have swollen to more and more unmanageable proportions, and have settled into more and more exact and cog-like relations with each other, teachers have found themselves required to " turn out a more uniform product," a process which is in its very essence utterly abhorrent to anyone with the soul of an educator.

Our State system of education has come to such an exalted degree of uniformity that a child in a third grade in Southern California can be transported to a third grade in Maine, and find himself in company with children being ground out in precisely the same educational hopper he has left. His temperament, capacity, tastes, surroundings, probable future and aspirations may be what you will, he will find all the children about his age of all temperaments, tastes, capacities, probable futures and aspirations practically everywhere in the United States, being " educated " exactly as he was, in his original graded school, wherever it was. School superintendents hold conferences of self-congratulation over this " standardizing " of American education, and some teachers are so hypnotized by this mental attitude on the part of their official superiors, that they come to take pride in the Procrustean quality of their schoolroom where all statures are equalized, and to labor conscientiously to drive thirty or more children slowly and steadily, like a flock of little sheep, with no stragglers and no advance-guard allowed, along the straight road to the next division, where another shepherdess, with the same training, takes them in hand. There is a significant anecdote current in school-circles, of an educator rising to address an educational convention which had been discussing special treatment for mentally slow and deficient children, and solemnly making only this pregnant exclamation, " We have special systems for the deficient child, and the slow child and the stupid child . . . but *God help the bright child!* "

Now it is only fair to state that this mechanical exactitude of program and of organization has been in the past of incalculable service in bringing educational order out of the chaos which was the inevitable result of the astoundingly rapid growth in population of our country. Our educational system is a monument to the energy, perseverance, and organizing genius of the various educational authorities, city, county, and state superintendents and so on, who have created it. But like all other complicated machines it needs to be controlled by master-minds who do not forget its ultimate purpose in the fascination of its smoothly-running wheels. That there is plenty of the right spirit fermenting among educators is evident. For, even along with the mighty development of this educational machine, has gone a steadily increasing protest on the part of the best teachers and superintendents, against its quite possible misuse.

Few people become teachers for the sake of the money to be made in that business ; it is a profession which rapidly becomes almost intolerable to anyone who has not a natural taste for it; and, as a consequence of these two factors, it is perhaps, of all the

professions, the one which has the largest proportion of members with a natural aptitude for their
lifework. With the instinctive right-feeling of human
beings engaged in the work for which they were
born, a considerable proportion of teachers have
protested against the tacit demand upon them by
the machine organization of education, to make the
children under their care, all alike. They have felt
keenly the essential necessity of inculcating initiative
and self-dependence in their pupils, and in many
cases have been aided and abetted in these heterodox
ideas by more or less sympathetic principals and
superintendents ; but the ugly, hard fact remains, not
a whit diminished for all their efforts, that the
teacher whose children are not able to " pass " given
examinations on given subjects, at the end of a given
time, is under suspicion ; and the principal whose
school is full of such teachers is very apt to give way
to a successor, chosen by a board of business-men
with a cult for efficiency. To advise teachers under
such conditions to " adopt Montessori ideas " is to
add the grimmest mockery to the difficulties of their
position. All that can be hoped for, at present, in
that direction, is that the strong emphasis placed
by the Montessori method on the necessity for individual freedom of mental activity and growth, may
prove a valuable reinforcement to those American
educators who are already struggling along towards
that goal.

This general state of things in the formal educa-

tion of our country is one of the many reasons why
this book is addressed to mothers and not to teachers.
The natural development of Montessori ideas, the
natural results of the introduction of " Children's
Homes " into the United States, without this already
existing fixed educational organization convinced of
its own perfection, would be entirely in accord with
the general, vague, unconscious socialistic drift of
our time. Little by little, various enterprises which
used to be private and individual, are being carried
on by some central, expert organization. This is
especially true as regards the life of women. One
by one, all the old " home industries " are being taken
away from us. Our laundry-work, bread-making,
sewing, house-furnishing, and the like, are all done
in impersonal industrial centers far from the home.
The education of children over six has already followed this general direction and is less and less in
the hands of the children's mothers. And now here
is the Casa dei Bambini, ready to take the younger
children out of our yearning arms, and sternly forbidding us to protest, as our mothers were forbidden
to protest when we, as girls, went away to college, or
when trained nurses came in to take the care of their
sick children away from them, because the best interests of the coming generation demand this sacrifice.

But as things stand now, we mothers have a little
breathing-space in which to accustom ourselves
gradually to this inevitable change in our world. At
some time in the future, society will certainly recog-

nize this close harmony of the successful Casa dei Bambini with the rest of the tendencies of our times, and then there will be a need to address a detailed technical book on Montessori ideas to teachers, for the training of little children will be in their hands, as is already the training of older children.

And then will be completed the process which has been going on so long, of forcing all women into labor suitable to their varying temperaments. The last one of the so-called " natural," " domestic " occupations will be taken away from us, and very shame at our enforced idleness will drive us to follow men into doing, each the work for which we are really fitted. Those of us who are born teachers and mothers (for the two words ought to mean about the same thing) will train ourselves expertly to care for the children of the world, collected for many hours a day in school-homes of various sorts. Those of us who have not this natural capacity for wise and beneficent association with the young (and many who love children dearly are not gifted with wisdom in their treatment) will do other parts of the necessary work of the world.

But that time is still in the future. At present our teachers can no more adopt the utter freedom and the reverence for individual differences, which constitute the essence of the " Montessori method," than a cog in a great machine can, of its own volition, begin to turn backwards. And here is the opportunity for us, the mothers, perhaps among the last

of the race who will be allowed the inestimable delight
and joy of caring for our own little children, a delight and joy of which society, sooner or later, will
consider us unworthy on account of our inexpertness,
our carelessness, our absorption in other things, our
lack of wise preparation, our lack of abstract good
judgment.

Our part, during this period of transition, is to
seize upon regenerating influences coming from any
source, and shape them with care into instruments
which will help us in the great task of training little
children, a complicated and awful responsibility, our
pathetically inadequate training for which is offset
somewhat by our passionate desire to do our best.

We can collaborate in our small way with the
scientific founder of the Montessori method, and can
help her to go on with her system (discovered before its completion) by assimilating profoundly her
master-idea, and applying it in directions which she
has not yet had time finally and carefully to explore,
such as its application to the dramatic and æsthetic
instincts of children.

Above all, we can apply it to ourselves, to our own
tense and troubled lives.   We can absorb some of
Dr. Montessori's reverence for vital processes.   Indeed, possibly nothing could more benefit our children
than a whole-hearted conversion on our part to her
great and calm trust in life itself.

INDEX

Adult analysis of children's problems, 143, 147, 154.
Animal training different from child training, 155.
Apparatus:
> Big stair, 72, 100.
> Broad stair, 100.
> Buttoning-frames, 13, 15, 55, 134.
> Color spools, 73.
> Explanation of, 99 ff.
> Geometric insets, flat, 76.
> Geometric insets, solid, 70.
> How to use, 67 ff., 91, 92, 99.
> Long stair, 100, 192.
> The Tower, 71, 100.

Age of children in Montessori schools, 8.
Apathetic child, the, 41 ff.
Arithmetic, beginnings of, 16, 100.

"Bad child," the, treatment of, 32.
Big stair, the. See Apparatus.
Buttoning-frames. See Apparatus.

Democracy, basis of Montessori system, 118, 187.
Discipline, 31, 141 ff.

Exercises, gymnastic, 146, 148; for legs, 112; for balance, 113, 115, 149.

Exercises, sensory:
> Baric, 65, 101.
> Blindfolded, 17.
> Color games, 74.
> Color matching, 73.
> Hearth-side seed-game, 110.
> In dimension, 16.
> In folding up, 107 ff.
> Instinctive desire for, 52-54.
> Not entire occupation of children, 68.
> Simplicity of, 54.
> In smelling, 64.
> Tactile, 59, 60, 100, 115.
> In tasting, 64.
> By use of water, 150, 151.
> By use of weights, 65, 101.

Family life, how affected by Montessori system, 121.
Freedom, 31, 103, 118, 119, 123, 131.

Gardens, value of, in child-training, 201, 204.
Geometric insets. See Apparatus.

Individuality, respect for, of Montessori system, 40, 93.
Interest, a prerequisite to education, 30, 94 ff., 190.

Kindergarten compared with Montessori system, 20, 173,

239